COST
OF THE
CALL

RAY SINES

WESTBOW
PRESS
A DIVISION OF THOMAS NELSON

WestBow Press books may be ordered through booksellers or by contacting:

WestBow Press
A Division of Thomas Nelson
1663 Liberty Drive
Bloomington, IN 47403
www.westbowpress.com
1 (866) 928-1240

ISBN: 978-1-4908-0859-8 (sc)
ISBN: 978-1-4908-1189-5 (e)

Library of Congress Control Number: 2013916830

Printed in the United States of America.

WestBow Press rev. date: 10/2/2013

TABLE OF CONTENTS

About the Author vii

Introduction xiii

Chapter 1:   The Call 1

Chapter 2:   The Promise 21

Chapter 3:   The Deviation 45

Chapter 4:   The Doubt... 60

Chapter 5:   The Answer 70

Chapter 6:   The Wait 84

Chapter 7:   The Revelation 108

Chapter 8:   The Confrontation 123

Chapter 9:   The Showdown... 144

Chapter 10: The Resolution 162

Chapter 11: The Reward.. 177

ABOUT THE AUTHOR

Ray Sines has been the senior pastor of the Erie Church of God, out of Cleveland, TN, for more than 30 years in Erie, PA. He graduated from Penn State at Erie with a BA in English, Creative Writing degree, in 1990. Ray was a staff writer for the Collegian where he wrote a monthly column titled: *Let's Talk*. He also served as the University Campus Ministry Chairman for seven consecutive years (four while attending college and three additional years after graduation).

Ray wrote a short story titled: *The Other Side of Harry*, which was published in the Church of God Evangel (Apr, 1990). Later he had a second short story published in Group Magazine, titled: *Howl-Loween Alternative* inside the back cover (Sep/Oct, 1997). Ray was a non-traditional student who completed college in four years, with a 3.33 GPA, while serving full-time at his pastorate.

Ray has three children, all of whom are married with families of their own, and all serve God faithfully. His wife, Bonnie, has served as the Lady's Ministry President for the past ten years, and she has taught every children's class from Kindergarten through Junior High.

Everyone who has left houses or brothers or sisters or father or mother or children or fields for my sake will receive a hundred times as much and will inherit eternal life.

—Matthew 19:29 NIV

No one takes this honor upon himself; he must be called by God.

—Hebrews 5:4 NIV

A special dedication to my wife and family who all made sacrifices because of the call God had placed upon my life. Bonnie stuck by me when many wives, I'm sure, would not have;

To my son and older daughter, who had to say goodbye to all their friends and class-mates, to leave private schooling and a social life they would miss the rest of their childhood to follow Dad into the unknown!

INTRODUCTION

Serving as senior pastor for the Erie Church of God for more than thirty years, during which time I also served seven consecutive years as the Protestant Campus Ministry Chairperson for the Pennsylvania State University in Erie, Pennsylvania, I have counseled many individuals, male and female, who felt called into a ministry. Talking with young students and not so young I would often ask: "How do you know you've been called into a ministry?" A few of the more interesting answers were:

"A prophesy was spoken over me and . . ."

"I had always felt, since a child . . ."

"My grandmother told me that one day I would become a preacher."

"I just feel God leading me in that direction."

"I've tried everything else and nothing has worked out. It must be what God wants from me."

It is not my purpose to expound upon particular "callings" or reasons to go into the ministry. I simply seek to impart, the hardships, agony and joy one may encounter who wholly accepts the authentic "CALL," in whatever area of the ministry he or she may become involved.

Neither am I suggesting, by any means, that the reader must experience the call as I did for it to be authentic, but rather to assure the reader that the authentic call will always be disclosed, in time by God, not man. God may confirm the call through others, but He seldom tells other individuals before the one to whom He calls. And, in addition, the authentic call will inevitably, in time, be acknowledged by the person's spouse and/or family. Although some spouses may not be able to bear the pressures involved, and bolt from a marriage relationship or even from God's blessings out of fear of the unknown.

I know a few individuals in particular whose lives were devastated because what they had anticipated as *"the call,"* turned out to be nothing more than false prophesy given by an emotional "do-good." One man, in particular, sold everything he and his family owned, except their car and clothing; moved to Mexico, to fall flat on his face because he had put his faith in another's statement rather than waiting for God's confirmation. Another had gone to Bible College, believing God wanted him to become a pastor, only to become disillusioned by the emotions he had earlier anticipated as *"the call."* He spent the next eleven years as an alcoholic, blaming God for messing up his life.

God has a specific plan for every individual to whom he calls and the revelation of this plan will come only from God, and God alone, not others. His plan may be for the individual to preach the Gospel of Christ (evangelize), to become a pastor of a church or teach, to prepare for missionary work, to become a minister of music, a youth pastor, etc. Then again, it may be God's desire for the person to continue in the present vocation while doing a personal in-depth study of His Word. Most often the latter may prove to be the case, especially during the early years of the call.

As a long-term pastor, I love my congregation, and they love my family and me dearly, but as far as ministering goes, I feel I have led more souls to the Lord simply by letting my light shine as a genuine Christian than I could ever expect to see in my church sanctuary on any given Sunday.

I have experienced some of the sweetest joys in my life since my pastorate began, but let me assure you, my family and I have also experienced much grief which followed my acceptance of the call. Nevertheless, according to Scripture, *"the gifts and calling of God are without repentance."* Romans 11:29 NIV

My desire is for each person to experience, in novel-like fashion, one, the unexpectedness of "the call," the physical, emotional and spiritual burdens brought on by the call, and the inherent costs, both material and spiritual, encountered after receiving and accepting the call; two, to have a subtle "how to" undercurrent flowing through each chapter; three, to be entertaining rather than sounding like an autobiography; and four, to be authentic in subject matter, events, dialogue, and imagery.

My wife, several years back, had purchased and read Joni, an autobiography written by Joni Eareckson Tada with Joe Musser, and it reappeared on the night stand. I began reading it because it was in reach of the bed when I couldn't sleep. The further I read, the more its style and structure fascinated me. It read like a novel with lots of dialogue yet had real people as characters. It showed, in story fashion, how Joni's terrible accident had left her a quadriplegic, and how she had overcome her struggle against quadriplegia and depression. I knew immediately how I desired to arrange the *Cost of the Call*.

I found this autobiography easy to write in the genre of a novel, and primarily because my life, since receiving the call, took on every aspect of an epic novel. The search for meaning of my vision became my quest in life. I needed to experience early assurance (supernatural events)—a foundation for personal spiritual strength which would later enable me to understand the vision. The closer I came to finding the answer, the more obstacles I encountered. Incorrect advice from others brought additional anxiety.

Once achieving an understanding of my vision, the battles became increasingly spiritual. Earlier conflicts were primarily material and physical, but then Satan fought my mind, the minds of my family and even the minds of those whom I highly respected in the security firm which I helped organize and loved. Final resolution brought about social changes, new anticipations, confirmations, and a permanent change of residency similar to the call God had placed on Abraham. *"Leave your country* [present location], *your people* [the people you fellowship with] *and your Father's household* [the company I helped start—my career] *and go to the land I will show you* [Erie, Pennsylvania]." Genesis 12:1 NIV

—Author

CHAPTER ONE

THE CALL

The vision, without question, was real. I saw myself standing behind the same oak podium, in the church I attended as a boy, speaking and pointing to a crowded sanctuary of faceless people. Silent words, spoken with authority, conveyed a grave message to each pale effigy. Each still, emotionless bust stood shoulder to shoulder in long rows, one behind another. The sanctuary was more than full. The captive audience extended beyond walls into infinity, both to the rear and on each side. It appeared as though I was preaching from the authoritative expression on my face and by the way I pointed my finger.

Three days earlier I had argued not to go to the Lay Evangelism seminar because I had already taken too much time from my job to work on the church. I packed a briefcase home every night, yet I knew Pastor Miller desired that a few laymen receive training in evangelism.

"I'd be glad to go if I had the money, but Nadine's check and mine together barely make ends meet as it is," Derry

Edwards said to Pastor Miller as he folded up a metal chair and placed it onto the rack.

Three of us stayed each Sunday night to dismantle the temporary church speaker system and remove the podium and chairs from the school gym. It had been nearly two years since we began worshiping in the Graham Elementary School after selling our old church and while waiting completion of the new church.

"I don't have the money either, but the church is dying without evangelism. No one has volunteered to go." I heard Pastor Miller respond as he lifted down one of the Bose speakers from its metal tripod stand. "It wouldn't cost that much if we shared the same room, besides we spent the past two years on nothing but the church building."

Their lack of money made me feel guilty as I monitored their conversation quietly stacking the folded chairs into the rack. I had just refinanced my home in Dale City a week ago and had taken $28,000 from my home equity to purchase five wooded acres on Sprigs Road to build our future dream house.

"I'll pay both your ways and all the expenses," I said, hoping to avoid committing myself to go under any circumstance. Even the word "evangelize" petrified me, much less learning how to witness to strangers.

"Ray, it wouldn't be right for you to pay all our expenses and not go along," Pastor Miller responded.

"That's right Brother," Derry agreed.

"I don't mind. You two go; then come back and teach the congregation."

We shoved the chair rack and podium back into the janitor's closet; then carried our portable sound equipment outside and set them on the sidewalk.

"Gimme' one good reason why you can't go," Derry said as he shook the school door to get the dead bolt to lock with the bent key.

"I have too much work stacking up and Bon . . ."

"Yeah Brother, Bonnie says all you do is work. Take a break," said Derry.

"The work will still be here when you get back," agreed Pastor Miller.

"Yeah, but we have to be out of the school by the end of the month, and I have the entire church electrical system to wire and . . ."

"Three days won't make that much difference," Pastor Miller said opening the Dodge church van to load the Bose speakers, stands, Yamaha mixer and amp.

"We have another building to activate this week," I argued.

"You mean to tell me the Vice President has to be there for every single building activation?" questioned Derry insistently.

"Alright," I said reluctantly running out of excuses. "But don't expect me to memorize both those sheets. Tonight is the first I've even looked at them."

After discussing additional details of the trip we finally said good night, and I walked to my company Malibu Classic where Bonnie waited impatiently with Rich and Shelly already asleep on the back seat.

"It's a-bout time. I thought you were going to spend the night with *Brother Miller* and *Mr. Derry Edwards*." Bonnie spoke each syllable of their names very distinctly as I opened the car door. "If you're not at Kastle, you're with them or working on that stupid church."

"I'm sorry. I didn't realize we had taken so long. After we put away all the chairs and everything else, Brother Miller wanted to go over an evangelism program. I'm not so keen on the idea, but I kind of promised I'd go with him," I said closing the door softly so it wouldn't wake the children.

"Go *where* with him?"

"To a seminar in Danville day after tomorrow," I said as I pulled out of the parking lot, and headed home.

"You know your mom is coming tomorrow for her eye appointment."

"She won't mind. She'll give you company while I'm gone. Dr. Huberman is only going to examine her eye anyway."

"You mean you're spending the *night*? Where *is* Danville anyway?"

"Yes. The southern tip of Virginia. Next to the North Carolina border. Two nights."

"You'd let Brother Miller talk you into anything."

I said little the rest of the way home. Bonnie thought the trip a total waste of money, but her condition made her more irritable than anything else. She was nearly seven months pregnant with our third child and her blood pressure had remained abnormally high all through her pregnancy. The hard metal chair hadn't helped matters either.

The next morning my older brother and his family dropped mom off around 11:00 am on their way to Disney World. They wanted to detour to Cape Hatteras for a day so they had already gone before I got home. I had some very pressing proposals to get out so I couldn't leave until almost two o'clock in the afternoon.

"Hello. I'm home." I yelled as I entered our split-level Colonial home in the suburbs going down the steps to the kitchen. "Hi Mom. How was your trip?" I asked loudly, giving Mom a big hug and kissing her cheek.

"Oh a little tiring, but mostly jittery thinking about my eye."

"Mom, he's only gonna' put drops in your eyes."

"What's that?"

"I said he's only going to *look* into your eyes. There won't be any pain."

"I just can't stand someone touching my eyes."

"How come Bo and Kay didn't stay?"

"Bo you say?"

"Mom, when did you change your battery last?"

"Battery?"

"Yes, your hearing aid battery. When did you last change it?"

"This thing must be dead again. I'm not hearing you right. This thing has been giving me a fit all week."

She took her hearing aid off and bounced it against the heal of her hand.

"Let me see it," I yelled.

I examined the switch and battery contacts then noticed that the tube was full of wax.

"The tube is clogged," I said loudly as my eyes scanned the kitchen for a paper clip or something small enough to fit into the plastic tube. Then I noticed the wire tie on the bread wrapper. It worked.

"Try it now," I yelled again.

She clipped it behind her ear and pushed the plug into her ear canal. Screech. Howl.

"It sure is loud now," Mom said happily, at half her previous volume. Thank you, Son. I don't know what I'd do without you boys."

"Is Bonnie lying down?" I asked while pouring a large glass of iced tea, bracing the refrigerator door open with my right knee.

"She's up on the living room sofa. She doesn't feel well. I come down to see if the steaks were thawed. We didn't know you'd be home this early."

"I thought I'd catch Bo and Kay before they left."

"They wanted to get to the hotel before dark. What would you like with your steaks?"

"Anything Mom," I said as I switched my iced tea to my left hand grabbing the mail from the table with my right. "There are left-over vegetables in the frig'," I said as I began to go up the steps. I wasn't sure if Bonnie was still upset from last night or not.

"Honey? You asleep?"

"No. My head's killing me, the baby's been kicking all morning and I feel sick."

"Do you want me to call Dr. Keller?"

"No, I'll wait for my appointment tomorrow."

"You sure?"

"Yes."

Bonnie's appointment was at 9:00 am and Mom's was at 1:00 pm. I made them both on the same day so I would only have to miss one day of work. Neither Bonnie nor Mom drives, and Dr. Keller insisted on seeing Bonnie every week since her blood pressure had climbed so dangerously high.

"Mom, would you like to go in with Bonnie? It'll be about an hour."

"I'll be alright," said Bonnie taking a deep breath gently pulling up on her stomach before opening the car door.

"I don't mind," Mom quickly injected. "Ray doesn't like sitting in there with all those women with big bellies."

"No, I want to check out that Bible bookstore across the street. I've been meaning to stop for the past three weeks."

"Come on Bonnie; take my arm. Big bellies don't bother me," Mom said jokingly.

An hour and fifteen minutes later Bonnie finally got out of the doctor's office. I had spent forty-five minutes in the bookstore and the balance in the car. "What did the doctor say?" I asked, knowing she would be more truthful since Mom had gone along.

"Her gynecologist wants her in the hospital," Mom said. "Her blood pressure is way too high."

"I'm not spending no two and a half months in the hospital," Bonnie insisted.

"Bonnie, your blood pressure is getting higher each week. If you have to go you have to go. Being stubborn doesn't help matters."

"That's just it. I don't *have* to go."

"What was the reading?" I asked in a milder tone, not to make it any worse, regretting that I had promised the Pastor and Derry I'd go to Danville.

"Two hundred over something. I don't know," Bonnie said angrily.

"Two hundred!"

"You both need to put more trust in God," Mom butted in.

"Let's grab an early lunch. We have two hours before Mom's eye appointment and I know a real good restaurant in Arlington." I didn't want another argument, much less in front of Mom. "They have really good egg rolls. It's less than fifteen minutes from here."

"I'll have a fortune cookie," Bonnie uttered barely audible.

"I could eat a bite," Mom said.

I took that as two yeses and headed for the China Inn, where I had gone many times for lunch. Kastle was just ten minutes away.

We took a long lunch and still had plenty of time to get to Dr. Huberman's office. I had made Mom's appointment with Dr. Huberman because he was not only a client of the company's, but the chief ophthalmologist at Arlington Hospital.

Bonnie insisted on waiting in the car when we arrived. I went in with Mom.

The small waiting room was crowded. A young boy, with a white bandage over his left eye, squirmed on his mother's lap, while his four-year-old sister rearranged the magazines into a road on the floor. An elderly woman, with a lavender dress, had what looked like half an egg taped over her left eye. Another older woman, with very little hair and a four-legged cane, had a bandage taped over her left eye which covered half of her nose. An elderly man and woman with an auburn wig both had on Ray Charles glasses.

I supported Mom by her right arm as she walked to the receptionist window.

"Mary Sines, to see Dr. Huberman," I said, watching that Mom didn't slip on the young girl's newly constructed road.

"Has she been here before?"

"No, I made the appointment through Dr. Huberman last month," I said.

"Oh yes, here it is. Just fill out the front side and have a seat Mrs. Sines. Dr. Huberman has had three surgeries this morning and he's a little backed up. It'll be about 45 minutes."

"That's OK," I assured her.

An hour and ten minutes later we left. Bonnie had taken a nap, read the paper and scanned every radio station. Mom wore her new plastic Ray Charles cover over her glasses to protect her dilated pupils. Her cataract surgery was scheduled for next month.

"We'd better hurry," Mom said. "Rich and Shelly will soon be getting out of school won't they?"

"No, we have plenty of time. Mom, I almost forgot, I need to go away for a couple of nights with Pastor Miller."

"Buying church furniture?"

"No, an evangelism seminar."

"You driving?"

"No, Brother Miller is taking the church van. Derry Edwards is going along and a couple from Reverend Stone's church. Pastor Stone can't go down until Friday."

"Bonnie and I will find plenty to do."

"I don't know how much doing I'll be doing Mom."

"You'll feel better after a good night's rest," Mom assured Bonnie.

"Mom, make sure she doesn't make a dozen trips up and down the steps, OK."

"Ray, you act like I'm a little girl. I'm thirty-three. Old enough to take care of myself."

"Then Mom can help take care of the *self* inside you."

Pastor Miller pulled into the driveway with the church van about 11:00 am and honked the horn. He had temporarily wired his Royce 40-channel CB into the van before coming over so he could communicate with others on the way to the seminar. He had the antenna clamped on top of the passenger's West Coast mirror and laid the CB on top the plastic engine cover. Derry was with him.

I kissed Bonnie and Mom goodbye then grabbed my grey Sampsonite suitcase from behind the door, the plastic bag with my goose down pillow which never spends a night alone, and a black marshmallow-leather bag which contained two Pierre Cardin suits and a couple Arrow shirts.

"See you sometime Saturday night," I said as I exited the air-conditioned house. "Give Rich and Shell a hug for me."

"Hey Brother, you spending two nights or two months?" Derry joked as he opened the side door reaching for my suitcases.

"You ought to be glad Bonnie didn't pack em' Brother," I rebutted.

"You guys gonna' debate all morning or are we ready to get on the road," Pastor Miller chimed in.

"All morning? You two have already used up the morning lollygagging around," I said as I pulled the side door shut and then lounged on the first bench seat. "Since you're already this late, how about stopping at Wendy's on the way out of Dale City. Some of us get up in the morning."

"We need to pick up Bill and Scott Ryman at Brother Stone's church first," Pastor Miller said. "You guys memorize the outline yet?"

"Memorize it! I didn't even read it," Derry answered. "Nadine had a month's chores for me to complete before I could even leave."

"I left my copy on the table," I said.

"I have a dozen more lying under the CB," Pastor Miller said eagerly.

We joked about the outline, our non qualifications, the Pastor's driving, Derry's lunch, Bill and his sixteen-year-old son riding with three clowns, our expectations after arrival, and discussed church building programs and several other items during the six-hour trip.

Each of us had dozed off a few times between conversations. Pastor Miller got sleepy after three hours at the wheel which woke us all in a hurry. Derry drove the next two and one-half hours, but since Pastor Miller knew Danville, he finished the remaining 35 minutes.

"Can you believe it, the Pastor got us here in one piece," I said opening the side door and stepping into the Holiday Inn parking lot.

"I may be here, but I'm not sure I'm in one piece," Derry said with a big yawn.

"Scott, did you ever hear anyone complain so much?" asked Harry.

"I just thank the good Lord I'm alive."

"I told you Scott was a good man, Ray," laughed Derry as he uncurled his lanky six-foot body out of the passenger seat into the parking lot.

"I'm ready for a long cool shower," I said as I pulled my suitcases and pillow out of the pile. A few cold glasses of ice setting on the dash would have put out more cold air than the van's air conditioner.

"That sounds like the best advice I've heard in hours," said Bill.

"You got that right," agreed Brother Miller and Scott.

Seminar registration lasted until 7:00 p.m. Nearly 170 laity and clergy had registered by the time we had showered and come down from our rooms. Bill and Scott met some people who had driven down from their church, so we made arrangements to pick them up after the seminar.

"I hadn't envisioned this big of a response," I said in a low tone to Derry as we stood in line to register and pick up our Evangelism-Breakthrough packets.

"Me either," Derry responded in like manner.

Pastor Miller seemed pleased, but made no comment. The registration table was placed in the doorway of the ballroom. People mingled from churches all over Virginia. We signed in, paid our fees, picked up our packets and walked into the ballroom which was now arranged like a sanctuary of tables instead of pews.

"This table OK?" I asked looking for Derry's and Pastor Miller's approval.

"Fine," said Pastor Miller.

"You want to be close to the iced tea vat or away from the front?" Derry asked since the table was next to the last row.

"No, I really just came to eat and to make sure you two get this stuff down pat," I said jokingly. Inwardly I had little interest of even being here much less learning how to witness.

About ten minutes later everyone was seated. The host pastor welcomed everyone and said grace, as our salads, rolls and coffee were being served.

Chicken breast or roast beef were our options. All three of us chose the chicken. After dinner, Doctor Leonard Albert, the only layman on the General Executive Board, explained, in his Boston accent, the importance of evangelism. He presented a pictorial image of the outline we had been given to memorize. I wondered how a person could be so vibrant after those mashed potatoes.

"There's no denying where he's from is there?" I said to Pastor Miller setting my empty coffee cup back on the table. "He sure made that outline come to life. Didn't he?"

"I'll say. You can tell his heart's in it," the Pastor said.

"We need to get him to come and speak at our church," Derry said, bending around me to catch Pastor Miller's expression.

Pastor nodded his head slowly without removing his eyes from Mr. Albert. Albert finished and everyone stood and applauded.

"He sure is good," I repeated to no one in particular.

"He sure is," came a reply from the table ahead of us.

After Albert left the stage the music committee chairman led a few choruses. His theme chorus was: "Bind Us Together." While repeating the chorus several times, he had everyone get out of their seats and shake hands with ten other people.

The singing ended and the host announced the night's guest speaker, who spoke on organized evangelism. He concluded with: "Good works will not get you into Heaven."

True, but we sure could use more workers, I thought. I couldn't help thinking about the many long hours of hard labor the Pastor, Derry and I had put into the church during the past two years.

I couldn't get the speaker's comment out of my mind. If I hadn't done anything, God would have still loved me and sent His Son to die for me. Inwardly, I began thanking the Lord for His awesome love. Before I realized it the Holy Spirit began blessing me like I had never felt before. My right hand went up almost automatically in praise to the Lord for what was happening to me. Tears of joy flowed down my cheeks. I was saying something. I didn't know what. It's like no one was in the room, except me and God.

The theme song was repeated as everyone dispersed to his or her separate rooms.

The Pastor, Derry and I shared a large room with two queen-size beds and a wall-mounted air conditioner.

"How do they expect us to memorize a two-page outline over night?" Derry asked. "My goodness, it's already eleven o'clock and breakfast begins at six. We'll have to memorize it in our sleep."

"I have a little tape recorder. We could each read the outline into the recorder; than let it play over and over again," Pastor Miller suggested.

"I heard somewhere if you put a speaker under your pillow your subconscious would record it while you sleep." I said not really wanting to put much effort into the outline. "I'll read first; then get a quick shower."

I showered and shaved. The auto-reverse recorder was repeating the monotonic outline word for word as I came out of the bathroom. Derry, lying diagonally across our bed was nearly asleep. Pastor Miller sat at the desk reading his Bible.

"Next." I hadn't realized how long I had taken.

"I thought you had drowned," Derry said sitting up quickly; then dashing into the bathroom before I could make a comment.

Derry showered then Harry. I flipped through the TV channels quickly to see what was on. Nothing. I glanced over the outline a couple times.

"I'm ready for some shut eye," Derry said as Pastor Miller walked out of the bath.

"Why don't we all have a word of prayer before we go to sleep?" Pastor Miller suggested.

We knelt by the beds. Pastor Miller led. I prayed silently. The evening sermon raced through my mind. I humbled my spirit before the Lord. I remember saying something like: "Lord, I'm so unworthy to be a witness for you" and then a peculiar feeling came over me which I find most difficult to express with words. I felt hallowedness at that moment as I had never felt before in my life.

I totally forgot about Derry and the pastor. I prayed with every ounce of sincerity I had.

I Wept.

Rejoiced.

I lay prostrate on the carpet. With my face in the shag carpet; eyes closed, I peered supernaturally into the future. I could see myself standing behind the heavy oak podium of the church, in Boynton, Pennsylvania, where I had attended as a young teenager.

The mystic scene was awesome. A unique wall-less sanctuary was filled beyond capacity with faceless empty people staring at the man behind the podium. The man was me.

At that moment Rev. Miller, without knowledge of my vision, began praying in tongues with resonant authority. Tears gushed from my eyes into the carpet, like miniature puddles on the floor.

The vision vanished. Silence filled the room after Pastor Miller's message in tongues.

I trembled and asked in silent fear, "Lord, what does it mean?"

Just then, almost as a mouthpiece of God, Rev. Miller interrupted my silent prayer and question to God with a prophesy: **"This day, I have *called you* to be an instrument for me; to learn of me; to teach my ways; . . . thus saith the Lord!"**

I dithered, not knowing if the Lord meant me personally or if he had called the three of us to evangelize. More bewilderment came as I pondered the vision. I prayed and begged for understanding. None came, at least not then.

I did not tell Derry, Pastor Miller or anyone else what had happened. I kept it to myself. I'm not even sure I wanted to know what it meant. One thing I knew for sure—God showed it to me, and He, alone, would have to show me what it meant.

I didn't sleep much that night. Hundreds of images flooded my mind. For a while I pictured myself in a far away mission field having to leave my family. Then I visualized the five-acre plot of wooded land on Sprigs Road, where we had decided to build our new home. I thought about my comfortable salary as electrical engineer; about Richard's and Shelly's private schooling. What if we had to give these things up?

I don't know when I dozed off. Before I realized it, I was grabbing over the night stand for the ringing phone that Bonnie must have moved. I was just about to shout: "Bonnie! Where did you put the phone?" when I knocked the lamp off the stand onto Pastor Miller's head; then I found the phone, hanging on the wall.

"Hello."

"Your wake-up call you requested. It's 5:45."

"Thank you." I wondered when I requested a wakeup call.

"What are you throwing lamps at me for?"

"To get you to stop snoring," I said. "Rise and shine, Brother," I said to Derry, as I yanked his covers off the bed onto the floor.

"Hey! I just got warm. What did you set that air conditioner at? Twenty below?"

"I thought Marines were tough," I said hurrying for the bathroom.

Pastor Miller looked like a large black bear wrapped up in his blankets in the middle of the bed beside us. Only the top of his head was visible.

"Don't use all the hot water," Derry bellowed getting up to turn the air conditioner off.

After breakfast everyone met in the ballroom again. Devotions were followed by Doctor Albert's teaching about two questions. He began:

"In your *pack ats'* you will find a 14k *gold* lapel pin in the shape of two question marks. *Don't just sit* there. Get them out and put them on. This pin could represent the two most important questions you will ever ask. And *wearing it* will remind you to *ask* them. Now the first question is simply: *May I ask you a question?* The second question is: *If you were to die tonight and stand before God, and He asked you, 'Why should I let you into my Heaven?' what would you tell Him?* The answer to this question will let you know what the individual is basing his faith on."

Dr. Albert mixed several skits, from people taken from the audience, with his lecture. He played every role from a fundamentalist to an agnostic. I laughed until my sides hurt.

About four o'clock the next afternoon the host pastor in Danville dismissed the seminar with prayer. We loaded the van and left for home. I drove.

"That was some seminar wasn't it?" I asked to solicit responses.

"It was awesome," Scott replied with nearly as much excitement as Leonard Albert.

"The best I'd ever gone to," said Pastor Miller.

"Well worth the money," Bill agreed.

"Our church would be filled in three weeks if we had him as a member," Derry said.

I had only driven about fifteen minutes north of Danville when I received an opportunity to test the questions. Channel 19 hummed with all kinds of discourse. I had never even talked on a CB before. I can't believe I even had the nerve to do what I did.

I keyed the mike and said, "Breaker one nine."

A trucker said, "Go ahead breaker."

"May I ask you a question?" I responded without thinking.

"Shoot, no handle," he answered.

"If you were to die tonight and stand before God, and God asked, 'Why should I let you into my heaven?' What would you say to Him?'"

Channel 19 got very quiet, for a moment, I thought a fuse had blown.

"That's a tough question to answer," he answered. "I don't know."

"Suppose you were to go out of here tonight, not knowing that Jesus had already died for you. That would be tragic wouldn't it?"

"This is no religion channel," bellowed an irate CBer'.

"Just trying to sow a good seed," I said. "Over and out."

To my surprise the trucker to whom I had asked the two questions responded to the outburst. "Careful good buddy. You don't know when you might need God some day."

CHAPTER TWO

THE PROMISE

It was nearly 10:30 pm when Harry, who had the final shift, pulled into my driveway. Derry handed my suitcases out, then tossed my pillow into my chest.

"Don't forget your pillow, Linus."

"Good night turkeys. See you in the morning." I laughed as Derry bumped the top of his Marine head trying to miss the side door that I had pushed shut with my foot.

"Good night Brother," Pastor Miller responded, laughing about Derry's thump.

The burglar alarm's entry warning beeper startled Mom, who had been lounging in the fully-extended recliner. She quickly jerked her feet downward and stood.

"Praise the Lord, Ray's home."

I entered the four-digit alarm code to turn off the alarm system, and noticed Bonnie lying on the sofa with two pillows propped behind her back. Her right leg was on the sofa and her left rested on the plush custom-made foot stool. She opened her eyes, but lay still.

"Hi Mom," I said as I came upstairs and kissed her cheek.

"Have you eaten?" Mom asked.

"Some snacks, but I'm not hungry," I answered while bending down to kiss Bonnie lightly on the lips. "Hi Bon. How are you feeling?"

"I'm OK. Tired. What did you do?"

"Do?"

"You never call me Bon unless you've done something. What's Brother Miller want you to do now?"

"Nothing. It was just a good seminar."

"I knew the moment you came in the Lord had blessed you by the shine on your face," Mom said.

I shared the two questions, the CB experience and all events except for my vision in the hotel room. We talked until Johnny Carson came on. Mom yawned.

"It's past my bedtime. I'm normally in bed by 9:30."

"I'm really tired. I'm going to bed," Bonnie said as she rolled off the sofa.

I helped her keep her balance as she walked toward the master bedroom. "Good night Mom," she said as we exited the living room.

"Good night, dear. I'm going to bed too," she answered, getting out of the recliner again.

"Night, Mom. I'll come back and get the lights."

Bonnie sat on the edge of the bed. I went into Shelly's bedroom, kissed her on the cheek, and pulled the covers up around her neck. Rich, twelve was snoring in his room.

I went downstairs to turn off the lights and on the way back up rearmed the alarm system. I decided to kneel by the sofa for a moment of prayer before going to bed to ask the Lord to comfort and protect Bonnie and the baby, and to reveal his will to us. I spent the next several minutes thanking him again for the many blessings he had given us. Just then, without expectation, a small, not even audible voice spoke to my spirit saying, *I have taken care of everything.* I lifted both hands toward the ceiling and praised the Lord. Tears ran down my face and dripped onto my T shirt. "Jesus, you are my Lord and my God. Let your will be done in my life," I prayed. I thanked Him again and again and praised His name. I wish words could express the assurance I felt at that moment.

I had prayed longer than I realized. The night light was on, but Bonnie had fallen asleep.

"Bonnie!" I awakened her. I was so anxious to share the good news I had received while praying.

"Go to bed. I'm tired," she said still half asleep.

"Honey, everything is going to be ok."

"I sure don't feel ok," she murmured.

"Bon, the Lord told me that he has taken care of everything."

"All right, now please go to sleep."

I wanted to say so much more, but I knew it would have to wait until another time. I pondered everything that had happened then prayed myself to sleep.

The next morning after Sunday School had ended, I, being the Superintendent, opened Morning Worship Service as on previous Sundays except this time I couldn't shut up. I began, sharing my testimony with the congregation about the CBer and the need for evangelism, but before I realized it, I had spoken for twenty minutes about basing your faith on Christ, and He alone.

Suddenly, without warning, a tall plump woman in a bright orange dress, whom I had never seen before, rushed to the make-shift altar we had built, crying openly to God for forgiveness. I didn't know what to do. I looked behind me at Pastor Miller, who was getting up from the metal chair on the platform.

"Good job Brother," he said quietly as he momentarily placed one hand on my shoulder.

I handed him the microphone, then retreated quickly to the chair he had been sitting in. My heart pounded as I again thought about the vision. That must have been it, I concluded, I was to speak this morning. But why my hometown church, I wondered? The school was not in the vision, I questioned every thought.

"God is moving in lives this morning. However big your need may be, God is bigger. Why don't you come and give it all to Him," the Pastor said opening the altar to anyone else who desired to come.

Some of the regulars responded. Bonnie and Mom remained with Derry and Nadine. Pastor Miller prayed with each person who had come, and was about to conclude the service when the woman in the bright orange dress requested permission to say something.

"Forgive me, but I must tell this [sob]. I left the house this morning to kill myself [sob]. I couldn't take it any longer. I live in the projects across the street. As I went by here I saw your church sign in front of the school door [sob] and I felt I should come in here first [sob]. I'm so glad I did. The message the other preacher gave was for me. Oh, thank you. Thank God."

She sat on the front row and continued to cry with her head bowed between her hands. Two ladies from the congregation went up and sat beside her to give her added support.

After church, she told me her name was Lois and asked if we would please pray that her children would not be taken from her. Pastor Miller jotted down her address and agreed to intercede on her behalf. We then said a special prayer for her husband and five children.

After leaving the church we took Mom for her rendezvous with Bo and his family on their way back through Virginia from Florida. Derry and Nadine had invited the pastor's family and us to a late dinner at their home after we returned.

We had barely gotten into Derry's front door when he started kidding Bonnie about the other preacher.

"That'll be the day," Bonnie said. "I'll never be a preacher's wife."

Derry wouldn't let it die. Soon Brother Miller chimed in. They loved to get Bonnie roused and continued all through the late afternoon meal. For awhile I played along until I saw that Bonnie was really getting upset. Her face turned red so I decided to cool it.

Underneath all the kidding and joking, throughout the day, I wondered if God expected me to preach, go to my home town church, pastor, teach or evangelize our community. After hearing Bonnie's comments, I was sure it wasn't preach. Besides, I concluded, if God wanted me to preach, he would have shown Bonnie too. He wouldn't tell me something without sharing the same message with her, especially since the Bible says that we two became one when we were married. Furthermore, I loved my position as Vice President of Engineering for Kastle Systems, my new home, and all my friends here. I wanted to ask Pastor Miller about the vision, but I knew this was not the time.

We went to the evening service directly from the Edward's. I marveled at how Pastor Miller could deliver such a serious message, after being such a cut-up an hour earlier. Still, within, I knew his message was from God. He motioned for his wife, Theresa, to come to the piano as he was about to give his altar call.

Theresa sat on the mahogany bench and sang in a soft sweet voice a favorite of hers by Dallas Holmes:

> *Rise and be healed, in the name of Jesus;*
> *Let faith, arise in your soul!*
> *Rise and be healed in the name of Jesus,*
> *He will make you ev'ry whit whole!*

Bonnie sat on the chair beside me. Her eyes were closed; her ruby cheeks were now smudged with tears. Her fidgeting and twitching made me think that she was suffering with pain. I was about to insist we go see her doctor immediately after service when she said:

"Let me out." She squeezed around my pivoted knees. "I want to be prayed for."

She stood in front of the blue carpeted platform we had constructed for a podium. Others followed suit. I stood behind her. Theresa repeated the song several times.

Pastor Miller removed the scented olive oil from the pulpit; unscrewed the cap and anointed each person's forehead; then he laid his hands on each of their heads, and prayed: "In Jesus name, be healed!"

The moment he touched Bonnie, she fell backward, almost taking me down with her. I grasped to catch her, but only caught her head as it was about to hit my feet. She was slain in the Spirit. I knelt by her head and prayed.

A few minutes later, she opened her eyes, her face aglow, and said very excitedly, "I'm healed! God healed me!

"Praise the Lord," I said softly.

I thanked the Lord and believed with her; then helped her up and back to the third row of folding metal chairs which had been arranged as pews. She couldn't wait to tell everyone how good she felt. When the healing service ended she took the opportunity. She confessed publicly what God had done.

"I feel good," she said with her face glowing more than I had seen it in a long time. "God has healed my blood pressure."

She repeated it two more times on the way home. I felt God was showing me something, but I didn't know what.

I was still very much uplifted the next morning when I went to work. My humming caught Bill Dietriek's attention as I walked past his office door toward the computer room.

"You get saved again?" he asked jokingly because two years previously I had shared my conversion experience with everyone in the company.

"No, God filled me with his Holy Spirit," I said as I turned into his office.

I tried to explain, but I'm not sure he fully understood. I kept my vision secret. Throughout the day I looked for any hint that would help explain its meaning. I found nothing, although I seemed to see only the good in each employee.

Bonnie's appointment was at 10:00 am the next day. I had stayed home to take her to her weekly doctor's appointment. All the way up I-95 she related how good she felt.

"He's not going to find any blood pressure," Bonnie said.

"You mean high blood pressure," I said.

"I mean my blood pressure is normal, and I'm going to have a little girl too," she insisted.

The moment we walked into the waiting room, Bonnie said to the nurse: "The Lord healed me. I don't have a blood pressure problem anymore." I was instantly embarrassed when four other women in the waiting room stared at her, then at me, the only male.

"We still have to check you," the nurse responded.

She walked with Bonnie into the little room on the left. The door remained open about two inches. Bonnie kept insisting that her blood pressure was normal. After the routine questions, the nurse stated: "There must be something wrong with this machine. Wait here; I'll go across the hall and get the other one."

She exited; crossed the waiting room; then rolled an older blood pressure testing apparatus into the room where she had left Bonnie.

"Here we go. Let's try this one," she said. "Now keep your arm real still on the table."

"That one won't work either. The Lord healed me," Bonnie insisted.

I became more embarrassed with each insistence.

"I must be doing something wrong," the nurse said. "Let me get Dr. Keller to check this. I'll be right back."

The nurse looked puzzled as she hurried out the door and down the corridor. A couple minutes later Dr. Keller followed her back. She spoke to Dr. Keller in a slightly subdued voice as they walked up the hall.

"It doesn't make sense. I keep getting 118 over 80," I heard her say with unbelief. "It's always been above 200."

They walked into the room where Bonnie waited.

"Well young lady, the nurse tells me you've turned into a sixteen-year-old since last week."

"The Lord healed me, Dr. Keller. And I'm going to have a girl too."

"Well let's see what we find."

I heard him squeeze several quick pumps of air then, after a few seconds, release of the air pressure.

"I see you have brought your blood pressure down."

"No, the Lord healed me. I've been telling the nurse, but she didn't believe me."

"Well I'll say one thing. Someone upstairs is looking out for you. After I finish with my other patient we'll do another internal. If everything is ok, we'll see you in two weeks."

My memory rewound to what the Lord spoke to me Saturday night: "I have taken care of everything."

Weeks passed by and Bonnie continued to get bigger, but remained inordinately healthy and active. I was putting ten hours per day in at Kastle and another five hours in the evening working on the church. The busier I became the less I speculated, as to what God required from me, although I searched my Bible each morning for an interpretation.

We didn't have an occupancy permit yet, but our small congregation desired to have Sunday services in the new building. Derry could only get his platoon commander to give him three days off because of a new class of recruits coming in, but between the Pastor and me, we managed to get enough volunteers to make it happen. Austin Morgan, the church clerk, Hank Simpson, a board member, and Earl Irvine, a carpenter, and all of our wives showed up for an all-out effort to make the new edifice ready for Sunday.

Volunteers put in more than 800 man hours in one week. Everyone had gone home except we three die-hards. Pastor Miller and I had just climbed out of the twelve-foot septic tank where we had wired mercury float switches into two large submergible sewage pumps. Derry peered back into the manhole with the trouble light to make sure we hadn't left any tools lay on top of the motors. We were mud from head to toes from silt that had oozed in between a faulty seal in the three piece concrete tank.

"Well, let's give it a test," I said while wiping mud from my forehead onto my shirt sleeve.

"All right!" the Pastor shouted.

Ring.

"We timed that about right didn't we?" I said as the outside phone bell rang. "Hey Derry, how about running up to the church and flushing all the toilets."

"You sure that rig will work, Brother?" Derry joked.

"It better. I sure don't envy going back down there again."

Ring.

"Derry, how about grabbing the phone while you're up there?" Pastor Miller asked.

"You two are worst then slave drivers," Derry yelled back as he began running toward the church which was 200 yards away.

Ring.

"DERRY, TURN THE WATER FAUCETS ON ALSO," I yelled.

Derry kept running, but waved his hand to acknowledge. The Pastor and I peered into the tank with the trouble light to wait for the bottom float to turn motor one on.

Ring.

"What time is it getting to be?" I asked. "My back feels like we've been underground for a week."

"If I can find my watch through all this mud. I put it in my pants pocket to keep from scratching the crystal. Oh no, the crystal's cracked. 9:05. I think," Harry replied.

Ring.

"Derry must be taking a complete bath outside before going into the church." I said, now lying on my stomach and staring into the manhole.

"I'm beginning to wonder," said Pastor Miller. "Maybe he's afraid of what Sister Agnus will do to him if he gets any mud on that new carpet."

"You got that right."

"The phone quit ringing."

"Here it comes."

A few minutes later the water pushed upon the bottom float.

"HOW MUCH LONGER," Derry yelled down from the church.

"ANOTHER MINUTE. FLUSH THE TOILETS AGAIN," Pastor Miller yelled back.

Derry pulled his head back inside the church door and quickly followed his latest instructions.

Whirl. The pump started.

"Let's close it up," I said thankfully.

"Alright," Pastor agreed.

"DERRY!"

"YES."

"TURN EM' OFF," I shouted.

We pulled the man hole cover into place and started up toward the church. Derry, bare-footed, quickly ran out and grabbed the water hose.

"Ray, quick! Let me spray you off. Bonnie called. It's time."

"Why didn't you tell me earlier?"

"I was going to, but you had me playing with the toilets."

Derry hit me full force with the cold water. After the sudden shock it felt rejuvenating. But my heart started pounding again the moment I remembered how fast Shelly had delivered. I had barely made it to the hospital in time, I remembered.

"I gotta' hurry. Did her water break yet?"

"Yes. Do you want us to go with you?"

"No. Just meet me at the Fairfax Hospital later."

I sat on the green velour seats of my Olds Ninety-eight, with my wet stained clothes, and then fish-tailed out of the gravel driveway onto the asphalt highway. Passing gear didn't kick out until eighty miles per hour. I made the twenty-minute trip home in eleven minutes.

It was 10:47 pm. when I bolted through the front door. Rich and Shelly were asleep. Bonnie's suitcase was sitting in the middle of the living room floor; she was in the bathroom fixing her hair.

"Bonnie! What are you doing? The baby doesn't care what your hair looks like."

"I guess you're going like that?"

"No. But I'll only be a minute." I answered, running past the bath to wake the children up. "Rich. Rich? Wake up. Your mom has to go to the hospital. Hurry and get dressed."

"Don't forget to call Buck to come and get Rich and Shelly," Bonnie said as I headed for Shelly's room.

"Shelly? Get up honey and call Buck."

I ran into the bathroom and stripped down to my underwear. I soaped the washcloth under the hot water and quickly scrubbed my face.

"Dad! Why do you want me to call Buck?" Shelly asked.

"You and Rich are going to spend the night with him."

"Why can't I sleep in my own bed?"

"Cause we have to leave. Now hurry and call."

"What's his number?"

"That's ok I'll call. Just hurry and get dressed."

I rinsed my face and dripped to the hall phone.

"Hello, Buck. It's time. I have to take Bonnie to the hospital. Can you come right away? Thanks."

I ran back into the bath and shampooed my head under the running faucet; rinsed; then dried on the clean white towel which I had already stained before making the phone call. I had wet clothes lying from the front door to the master bedroom. Coming out of the bathroom, I remembered that I needed to call the hospital to let Dr. Keller know we were on the way.

"Hello. Fairfax Hospital. Yes, this is Bonnie Sines. I mean her husband. She's on the way. Dr. Keller said to call before the baby came. The water is broken. We'll be right there. Thanks. Bye."

"Come on BON! Hurry up!"

"You going in wet underwear?"

"No. I'll be right out."

"I hope with clothes," Bonnie laughed.

The doorbell rang.

"Rich, let Buck in," I yelled from the master bedroom. "You guys listen to Buck and Linda. I'll see you tomorrow ok? Thanks Buck."

"Tell Mr. Cool I'll see him tomorrow, Bonnie. The kids will be fine," my nephew, Buck said.

Finally, I had clean dry clothes on and the formerly white towel from the bathroom was now brown. Bonnie was standing in the living room beside her suit case holding her back with one hand and the stair rail with the other. "Honey! Wait! I'll help you down the steps."

"I wasn't going anywhere."

"Put your weight on my arm."

I helped Bonnie into the car, and ran around the car to get in.

"Ray, get my suitcase. And the door is standing wide open."

The car had been idling all this time. Bonnie had another contraction before I even got my seat belt fastened.

"Uh!"

"How close are they?" I asked.

"Two minutes."

"TWO MINUTES! Why didn't you have the baby, and then call me," I growled. Don't you remember how fast Shelly came?"

The tires squealed as I backed out of the asphalt driveway, sending my neighbor's empty metal garbage can rolling down the street.

"Slow down," Bonnie said.

"Honey, it is 30 minutes to Fairfax. I have to hurry."

I turned my four-way flashers on and sped out Davis Ford Road. The first light was green. The second was red. I slowed down; saw there was nothing coming; then ran the light; then headed up I-95.

I laid on my horn and flashed my high beams up and down. The sparse three-lane traffic split like the Red Sea. I glanced down at the speedometer now and then, but didn't see the hand. Bonnie's pains came closer and closer. They had quickly gotten to 50 seconds apart.

"Thank God, Fairfax two miles," I said with a sigh.

"OH, UH," Bonnie answered with a severe pain.

Honk! Honk!

"Come on lady, move over!"

She refused to heed so I passed her on the exit ramp, throwing gravel as I went around her. She honked her horn and put on her high beam lights, but I was soon so far ahead of her that the lights didn't bother me. Besides, I had quickly moved my mirrors so her light did not blind me. Before long I was heading into the hospital.

The hot tires squealed as I turned into the emergency entrance, and the car jolted as I slammed the shifter into park. I threw open the door, and ran into the emergency room demanding a wheelchair, in a loud authoritative voice.

"Hurry! My wife's having a baby in the car."

An orderly snapped open a chair and hustled to the door. We unloaded Bonnie into the wheelchair. The orderly hurried up the ramp as I quickly sped the car into a parking spot. I almost shoved Dr. Keller, who had just arrived, through the door as I hurried back into the hospital.

"I thought I left instructions for you to wait until I called back, before coming to the hospital."

"You did, Dr. Keller, but when my wife decides to have a child she doesn't wait for anybody," I answered. "I barely made it to the hospital in time for our second child. She started to come in the wheelchair."

"Well let's go have a look," said Dr. Keller.

We hurried to where they had taken Bonnie. We had made all the arrangements previously, thank God. Dr. Keller sounded a bit upset, but I was just thankful to have Bonnie in the hospital, and that we made it here safe. I glanced at my watch and saw it was 11:28 pm. My knees felt a little rubbery. We rode the elevator to the eighth floor together.

"Wait here. I need to examine her," demanded Dr. Keller.

"Ok Doctor."

Dr. Keller hadn't been in there a full minute until he hurried back out.

"I've sent for the anesthesiologist. Dr. Liechman. He's on his way up now."

"Can I wait with my wife, Dr. Keller?" I asked knowing that I had already made arrangements to be with Bonnie during delivery.

"Yes, but you'll have to step out when Dr. Liechman gives her the spinal block."

"Thank you," I said as I quickly jumped up from the chair and went into where Bonnie was lying.

"Sir you can't be in here. We're getting ready to give your wife a shot," scolded a mean-looking nurse.

"Dr. Keller said I could stay until Dr. Liechman arrived," I responded ignoring her glaring eyes and walking over to take Bonnie's hand. "How's it going Bon?"

"Oh! R-a-y. I just want to have this baby. It hur-t-s."

"Mr. Sines, you are going to have to leave now. The anesthesiologist is here," barked the nurse again.

"UH!" Bonnie had another contraction.

I left the room and sat in a chair just outside the door. It seemed Bonnie was having a contraction every second. I felt so helpless. My silent prayer count must have been up to nearly thirty by now. I cringed at every agonizing cry Bonnie gave.

Shortly Dr. Keller came back through and went in the room with the anesthesiologist. Then two orderlies brought an empty bed in. Dr. Keller came out.

"What's happening?" I asked.

"We're taking her to delivery. She has to have natural birth," Dr. Keller explained rapidly. The spinal tap is too dangerous to give because her contractions are too close together."

"I don't understand, Doctor."

"She won't hold still long enough," Dr. Keller said.

"Put these on and follow me." Dr. Keller handed me a gown, a mask and a pair of footie's. "Wash your hands with that pink soap over there. Don't touch the door handles with your hands when going in."

I quickly followed all his instructions and followed him into the delivery room.

"Well Mr. Sines, it seems you know your wife pretty well. When she decides to have a baby she doesn't fool around." Dr. Keller remarked as the orderlies lifted Bonnie onto the delivery bed and two other nurses fastened her feet in stirrups. I prayed again for her pains to ease. I wanted to say I told you so, but I was too busy wiping the sweat from Bonnie's forehead and squeezing her hand.

"The head's out. And here come the shoulders. You got your girl." Dr. Keller said almost astonished as he clipped and tied the umbilical cord then held the bluish, slimy newborn up and slapped its leg.

"Whaa."

"A good set of lungs too," Dr. Keller said. "Here, Mr. Sines. Hold out your hands out. She won't break."

I held the tiny crier for a few seconds; then showed Bonnie.

"I told you," said Bonnie with a big smile on her face. "Thank you Dr. Keller."

"Don't thank me. You did all the work. I wouldn't even had to have been here. If you feel this good tomorrow girl, you can go home in the morning."

"Can the baby go too?" Bonnie asked.

"That's not up to me. The pediatrician has to make that determination," said Dr. Keller.

"She is so little," I marveled aloud.

"We have to clean her up now and get her under the lights so she stays warm," said Dr. Keller as he took little Cindy from my hands and placed her in a little stainless steel tub under two brownish looking lights.

"You'll have to wait in the outer room now Mr. Sines," Dr. Keller said. "We have to clean your wife up. Cindy will be down the hall in front of the glass window in about ten minutes."

"Bon, I'm going to go make a few phone calls and see if I can find Derry and Pastor Miller. I told them to meet me up here. I'll see you in the recovery room." I said as I kissed Bonnie on the forehead.

"I don't have to go to the recovery room . . . ," Bonnie said to impress the Doctor even more.

"For about an hour, Mrs. Sines. Then they'll take you to your room," Dr. Keller cut in.

"Alright." She was a bit too weak to argue.

"See you in a little bit hon." I hurried out to find a phone; to spread the good news.

"Mom! Bonnie had the baby . . . . A girl . . . . Six pounds; thirteen ounces . . . . I don't want to talk long; I have more calls to make . . . . Love you. Bye bye."

"There he is at the pay phone," Derry nudged Pastor Harry as they came down the corridor.

"Hello. Udell? Bonnie had her girl . . . . A little over six and a half pounds . . . . Right now it is just Baby Girl Sines . . . . Tomorrow . . ."

"Hey Brother," Derry interrupted.

"Just a second Udell, someone is trying to get my attention." I held my hand over the mouthpiece then turned to acknowledge Derry and Pastor Miller. "A Girl. She'll be in the window in a few minutes."

"Udell, Pastor Miller and Derry Edwards are here. Call Nancy and Patty, ok? . . . Ok. I'll call back tomorrow sometime . . . . Bonnie wants Lee Anne; I want Cindy Rae. We don't know yet. Well, I have to make some more calls . . . . I'll let you know as soon as we decide. Bye bye."

"Timing was pretty close, huh Brother?" Pastor Miller said.

"Too close. My heart is still thumping like a tom-tom."

"Did you get to stay in with Bonnie the whole time?" Derry asked.

"Yes."

"We got interrogated by some nurse drill sergeant on the way in here. She said we were not allowed in here after 9:00 pm. The Pastor told her how far we had driven; then she gave orders: **ten minutes only**!"

"How's Sister Sines doing?" Pastor Miller asked.

"She's doing real well. The anesthesiologist didn't even have time to give her a shot, so she had a complete natural birth."

"Ray, they opened the curtain on the baby window a little piece!" Derry said in a loud whisper.

We all walked quickly and quietly to the window.

"Look there. Baby Girl Sines. Isn't she tiny?" I said proudly.

"Where did she get that red hair?" asked Derry. "Bonnie's blonde and you have dark brown hair."

"Bonnie's mom, her brother and her one sister all have red hair."

"Brother Sines, we had better take off. I'm so happy for the both of you." Pastor Miller said.

"I don't know about the baby, but the doctor said Bonnie could possibly go home tomorrow."

"Tomorrow! No. They keep them at least three days. The military keeps them a week," Derry said.

"That's what the doctor said in the delivery room," I assured him.

"Come on Brother Edwards, we have to go. It's going on fifteen minutes," Pastor Miller reminded him.

"Good night guys. I'll keep in touch," I said.

After Derry and Harry went down the corridor, I went into the recovery room to tell Bonnie good night.

"Sir, you're not supposed to be in here," the nurse on the other side of the door said.

"I'm just going to tell my wife good night. I'll only be a minute."

"Only a minute."

"Bonnie, you asleep?

"No, I was sitting up and they made me lie down. They can't understand why I'm not suffering or how I feel so good. One nurse even asked me if I had the baby yet."

"Well go to sleep and rest up for tomorrow."

"Did they put the baby in the window?"

"Yeah. She really is a cutie. Bright red hair."

"Mr. Sines? You'll have to leave now," the nurse said in a polite, sweet authoritative voice.

"Bon, I got to go. See you in the morning about nine." I kissed her and left for home.

The next morning I got Rich and Shelly off to school; then arrived at the hospital about ten after nine. Bonnie was in a private room, dressed, sitting in the chair and raring to go home.

"Good morning honey," I said as I kissed her lips. "Has Dr. Keller been in yet?"

"Yes. He said I could go home at 11:00. I hope the baby can go too."

"Did you see her yet this morning?"

"Yes. I fed her at seven. You ought to see her eat."

"Has the pediatrician been . . ."

"No, but a nurse is coming back at 9:30. We have to decide on the name," She said with an urgent tone. "I still like Lee Anne."

"Lee Anne sounds like a middle name before a first name. What about Cindy Leanne?"

"Yeah!"

"That's it then. Cindy Leanne."

Dr. Levine, Cindy's pediatrician, finally came at 11:30 am and gave his okay to take Cindy home. A nurse pushed Bonnie and the baby, in a wheelchair, from the room and they waited with me at the cashier's window.

"In and out in less than twenty-four hours. That's pretty good," The cashier acknowledged as she went over the paperwork.

"That's kind of unusual isn't it?" I asked.

"No, we are seeing this more and more," the nurse answered. "Let's see. You're insurance coverage is $500, and the total bill comes to $496.53. It's all covered. Just sign where I marked a little red x."

Immediately the thought came back to me: *I have taken care of everything.* I reiterated this to Bonnie as we drove slowly down I-95 towards home.

CHAPTER THREE

THE DEVIATION

Designing electronic circuits, providing computerized access and egress into high-rise office buildings, and developing a new card reader didn't have my undivided attention it held for the past ten years. Work orders and floor plans of new office buildings were all over my desk, but my focus would constantly drift to doing God's work. I would feel guilty if I didn't give Kastle my undivided attention yet when I tried to, I would feel even more guilty for putting God off. I would often step into the back of a computer rack to wire in or test a new building's circuit, but would spend as much time there, hidden from everyone, in prayer as I did performing my electronic duty.

Ever since my father had died, Gene Samburg, Kastle's President had been more like a big brother to me then my boss. He helped council me after an affair I'd had several years ago. In fact, for a few hours, Gene practically filled in for my father. He trusted me and I highly respected and trusted him. Our goals from the time we both resigned from Westinghouse

Electric on the same resignation were to make Kastle the largest and best high-rise office building security company in the world. And, in so doing, both of us, in time, would become millionaires. I had the electronic head knowledge from tech school combined with four years military electronics training, yet Gene, an electrical engineer from Cornell University, had taught me how to actually design my very first circuit. He made it so easy to understand that from the moment the light finally clicked on in my brain I had felt there was nothing I couldn't tackle electronically. Gene showed me how to break down the most complex circuit into several simple circuits. I no longer viewed office building security as one massive system, but rather many small individual circuits tied together. Over the years the security circuits became more and more complex utilizing very high-tech sensory-devices, but to me they had become as easy as adding another letter to the alphabet. Our systems even monitored building's HVAC systems, fire alarms, sprinklers, and whatever else a building engineer desired for us to monitor electronically. Our most recent engineering venture was to control building elevators remotely after hours via our computers in Arlington, Virginia. During those hours only certain elevators would permit access to a tenant's authorized floor(s) which was predetermined by the building owner and tenant.

I received a very lucrative salary and expense account, leased a new company car of my choice every three years, had full medical coverage which was totally paid by the company and many other company perks. But ever since my Danville experience nothing remained the same. The vision God had given me begged to be understood. After several weeks of carrying the burden alone, I made up my mind to share my vision with Pastor Miller this coming Sunday after church.

We went out to eat after church as we did nearly every Sunday. After filling up on all the shrimp we could eat at the Chesapeake Bay Seafood House, in Woodbridge, I decided to tell Pastor Miller and Brother Edwards about my vision. We were at one end of a long table; our wives and children were at the other. Several people who had previously joined us for dinner had recently left, so I perceived this an opportune time to share my vision in the hotel room and how it tied into Lois coming to the Lord.

"Do you think God wants me to go to Boynton?" I asked Pastor Miller as Derry listened attentively.

"No! Often God will use something that you are very familiar with to get your attention. Or to show you something," Pastor said.

"Does God want me to be a preacher?" I asked again, hoping his answer would be no.

"God may want you to do something that doesn't even pertain to your vision at all," Derry injected.

"Like what?"

"Maybe by seeing a different church He wants you to do different work," Derry answered.

"Derry you're really confusing me."

"No! Maybe He wants you to start an all-Christian company and do the same thing that you're doing now."

"You never know it could be something like that," Pastor Miller agreed.

"You could hire all Christians. They would all pay tithes. You would be blessed and the church would be blessed at the same time," continued Derry relentlessly.

"I don't know. I just don't feel it's in security," I answered hesitantly. "Anyway I wouldn't even think of competing with Gene at Kastle. Gene and I are like brothers. I'll never go against him."

"You wouldn't have to compete. You could do all the jobs that Kastle doesn't want to do," Derry said holding to his reasoning like a pit bull.

"Kastle doesn't do homes. And I know several people who could use a home security system," said Pastor Miller.

"I don't know. I'd really have to think about it."

A week later, during break around 10:00 o'clock, I was reading *"Our Daily Bread's"* devotion for the day which dealt with responsibilities and blessings of laymen, written by Dr. De Haan. I learned that laity had come from a Greek word meaning "workers of God." Then an idea flooded my mind. Maybe God does want me to start a Christian company— **Workers of God**. It had a good ring to it. I spent the next hour jotting down possible names for a company. Later that night after Bonnie had gone to bed I came up with Laity Enterprises, Inc. I decided not to use the words "security" or "systems" because I felt by using the word "enterprises" I could do other things under the same corporate name if it turned out that God wanted me involved in another line of work. Everything seemed to click. I became almost as excited as the day Gene and I conceived Kastle Systems, Inc. while we were in our Westinghouse office in McLean.

The next few weeks all my efforts were spent researching the ins and outs of becoming incorporated. I decided to incorporate in Delaware since, there, I only needed three officers to form a corporation. I would be the President, Pastor Miller the Vice President and Bonnie could be the Secretary. Without hesitation I picked up the phone that Monday morning and called Aaron Fodaman, a lawyer friend of mine whom I had put a fire alarm system in his home that Kastle had provided. After a long conversation Aaron reluctantly agreed to draw up the paperwork and get the corporation process underway.

Two and one half weeks later the corporate seal arrived with the impressive minutes book done in a royal blue leather binding. I stared at the gold seal on the front of the book for several minutes. I couldn't believe it. I had just set up my own company. I was excited yet I didn't feel the inner joy I had anticipated, especially after Bonnie rejected the idea of being Secretary to something she knew nothing about, even if it was "only" a title.

I spent the next day opening personal lines of credit with several distributers I had become acquainted with over the last ten years. After lunch I ordered a computer/alarm printer from Ademco, a supplier I had been very familiar with on Long Island, New York. Late that afternoon when I finished at Kastle, I drove a few blocks into Arlington; to examine the facility of an answering service that I felt could monitor the computer printer 24/7. After an hour we signed a contract and they agreed to learn the operations of the computer. First thing the next morning I ordered the phone service to the computer and a company telephone to be placed on my desk at Kastle. I had worked with every telephone man in our building so acquiring the phone service was the easiest part of it all.

After the Laity phone arrived, I explained to Gene that I was doing this on the side and that I desired to secure homes of building owners who wanted quality systems installed in their homes. Gene didn't seem too happy but went along with the idea as long as it didn't interfere with my work at Kastle. On his way out of my office he said rather sarcastically, "Welcome to new tax liabilities."

Within four months I found myself with more work than I could handle. Since Laity phone calls were taking much of Kastle time, and with Gene getting more aggravated on a regular basis, I decided to give Kastle a 30-day notice and go full-time with Laity. Gene was hurt with my decision to leave Kastle, but he figured it was coming and being the prudent businessman that he was, made provisions to fill my position.

He bought out the lease on my Malibu Classic I had been driving, and gave it to me as a going away severance.

Within a week after resigning from Kastle I rented an office in West Springfield, Virginia and hired two men full-time from our church that had been helping me in evenings. I planned to hire only Christians and as many as possible from our church. Laity soon expanded to seven employees which now included one installer and a secretary from our neighbor church where Rev. Stone pastored. I had a good client reputation from the building owners, so we had about all the jobs that we could handle for the time.

Six months later Gary, one of Kastle's salesmen, offered to sell part-time for Laity for a ten percent fixed commission. Gary's first sale was a small office building in Maryland which I initially refused because I felt it competed with Kastle, but Gary assured me that the owner only wanted to secure the perimeter with a keyed entry so I agreed. This was the largest contract we had landed to date so I flew Derry in from Weatherford, Texas in order to complete the job in a timely fashion. Derry had recently retired from the Marines, and he and his family had moved to his hometown in Texas, even though none of us wanted them to leave Virginia. My ulterior motive was to possibly get Derry to move back to Virginia although I didn't share this with him. Derry agreed to come not because we needed him to pull wires, but because he missed the church and all the fun we had together.

"I knew you guys couldn't run a company without me," Derry said jokingly as soon as I picked him up at Dulles International Airport.

Laity in no time was billing more than $10,000 per month and most of those accounts elected to be monitored on our central computer system which generated an additional yearly income of $300 a year per account. Our accounts receivable quickly soared to more than $60,000. The installers were receiving good bimonthly paychecks and my secretary turned into a top-notch office manager. Laity had grown well into six-digit figures the very first year. My confidence grew because I felt God was really blessing our endeavors.

After only one and one-half years of remarkable success the bottom started dropping out of the economy. In no time Laity's accounts receivables stalemated for more than three straight months. Suppliers began calling for payments. Some even switched us to cash-only basis.

Rev. Stone, our District Church Overseer, then approached Harry and I with an offer to buy into Laity and become our Treasurer, for which he would give the company a badly needed $10,000. He felt that Laity was only in a slump, but still had great potential to make lots of money. After much discussion Harry and I elected to take Rev. Stone up on his offer although nothing had been documented or signed. The ten grand temporary bailed us out, but the money didn't last long because the economy remained in a long slump. Accounts receivables came in slower and slower, with several accounts more than 90 days in arrears. I hated to lay off any of my employees because I felt a layoff would drastically affect our struggling church finances as well as our company image. We were already four payments behind on our new church building and as a Board we were constantly trying to work with the bank, not knowing how we would ever get caught up. During the same time Rev. Stone got cold feet and wanted his investment returned. Harry and I had both heard the words "buy into," but Rev. Stone insisted it was only "a loan." I quickly realized that Laity, as any business, could not be run on trust even if everyone was a Christian. I was forced to take a second mortgage on my home to reimburse Rev. Stone, as I wanted no hard feelings between us.

Trying to make Laity profitable grew more and more stressful as days turned into weeks, and weeks into months. I laid off several employees and chose to keep only one crew and my secretary. I even had to temporarily, borrow from funds that were in escrow for IRS employee withholding taxes. It grew more and more difficult to separate church financial stress from Laity financial stress. Some days I didn't know whether I was coming or going.

The Church Council decided to renovate the church parsonage and sell it as a measure to stop foreclosure on the church which had now escalated to ten payments in arrears. The bank agreed to handle the sale of the parsonage, if we came up with a buyer. I assured the Council and the loan officer at the bank that I had a buyer for the parsonage. I had previously talked to Gary and he agreed to buy the parsonage if we would renovate it and make changes to his liking.

The Council agreed so Gary gave us immediate cash to make one church payment to appease the banker and the money needed to begin renovation with additional payments as progress proceeded. To overcome my depression from Laity's lull, I began taking afternoons off to act as foreman for the parsonage renovation, quickly losing all interest in Laity Enterprises.

It didn't take long to realize I was putting more time at the parsonage than time spent at Laity. During evenings and on Saturdays my nephew, Buck and occasionally a man or two from the church would help as often as they could.

Today was the day we all agreed to move Pastor Miller's furniture into the apartment the church had rented for him and his family in Dale City. We couldn't do any more renovating until all of Pastor's furniture and possessions were removed in order to remove the basement stairs and install a spiral staircase which Gary had ordered. This would allow us to relocate the entrance to the front of the house.

"Don't blame Brother Miller for the large church debt," I said to my nephew, Buck, as he carefully backed his new Chevy C-10 into Pastor's rutted driveway. "It's not his fault half the people got cold feet during the building program and left the church. If you'll remember, when I became a member of the Church and Pastor's Council, everyone was going to help build. There were two carpenters, a bricklayer and a dozer operator. Where are they now?"

"I know, but every service all I hear is money, money, money," said Buck.

"The money doesn't go to Pastor Miller. Just last month Theresa told me she had to get Marshall's tennis shoes on her MasterCard because they had no money. Oh, here comes Hank up the road. It's hard to believe that old truck of his still runs."

"You know Hank. He'd glue the engine in if he had to."

Pastor, Buck and I would often kid Hank about his old pickup, but it was always in fun. Hank insisted on getting the last bit of life from everything. The screech of Hank's brakes sent a shiver up my back. Something under the truck clanked when he finally found reverse. I chuckled again at his truck. "Good morning, Hank. Did you bring the coffee?"

"Coffee! I barely got here myself. Is the preacher up yet?"

"I saw a light come on as we backed into the driveway," Buck answered.

"*Ya'* know, I kinda' hate to see this *ole* place sold," said Hank as he slammed his truck door three times to get it to stay shut.

"Not me," I said, "I just thank God we have a buyer as lenient as Gary."

"Let's see if there's any way to get one of our trucks closer to the back door," said Buck. "I hate the thought of lugging all that stuff down those rickety steps."

After walking around to the back, Buck and I both became convinced that no contractor had built this house. The bottom rear windows sloped inward nearly 15 degrees, the front entrance was on the back rear corner, and what appeared from the road to be the front entrance was actually the basement entrance which led to a "storage" room.

"Come on in," Pastor Miller said through a torn window screen in the kitchen. "Theresa has the coffee on. Help yourselves to the doughnuts."

Pastor devoured two coconut-covered doughnuts as we kidded him about his size 42 brown polyester pants which were already too small. His stretched leather belt, with its four-inch Western buckle, strained to keep his fly shut.

Suddenly Marshall, Pastor Miller's 4-year-old, bolted out the bedroom yelling, "Wa'cha doin'? Are we movin' to our new house today?"

"You sure are," I answered as he jumped into my arms.

"Are we sleepin' there tonight?"

"Not you. You have to sleep in the dog house."

"No I don't! Do I, Daddy?" His face soured as his body went limp and slid out of my arms.

Pastor laughed.

"Let's get the trucks loaded," snorted my nephew. "I only get one Saturday a week. You guys would stand here and gab till noon."

"Let's do it," agreed Pastor Miller. "Take the beds first. If we don't get it all, at least we'll have a place to sleep."

We carried load after load. Filled the trucks. Drove to Dale City, unloaded and returned. Theresa and the children stayed at the new apartment to make beds, and unpack dishes. Hank's injured back didn't allow him to do much lifting, so he organized and packed the trucks as Buck set boxes onto the tailgates. Pastor and I packed boxes and set them at the foot of the stairs for Buck to carry to the trucks.

The accumulation was overwhelming. I carried scratched wooden bed rails, boxes, clothes that I would have given to the Salvation Army, dishes, lamps with torn shades, two Cabbage Patch dolls with bewildered looks on their faces, a nine-inch color TV, blankets, and stacks of papers, books and magazines.

"How in the world did you stockpile so much in such a little house?" I asked Pastor Miller.

"It wasn't easy."

I wasn't sure if he meant it wasn't getting it into the house or easy acquiring it. Most of the house looked like it had been furnished from garage sales, although an occasional luxury item would avail itself.

It was nearly 2 o'clock when I began taking down the Donald Duck curtains in Marshall's room. The rod was bent, so I hit up on it with the heel of my hand. Rod and curtain both crashed to the floor as the window shade went slap, slap, slap. The sun shot through the dirty window into my eyes. Then I realized the glare was coming from a mirror on a motorcycle.

"Brother Miller, Whose Gold Wing is parked out beside your shed?"

"Oh!" Pastor paused for a second. "Mine."

My tongue couldn't find words for a few seconds. Just a week ago Theresa had told me their MasterCard had reached the limit. Her words now echoed in my ears, "Ray, we owe more in monthly bills than we gross."

"How can preachers afford new motorcycles?" I asked in jest, but hoping for a logical explanation.

"The first payment isn't due for nearly three months," Pastor answered slowly from the master bedroom.

A few moments later Pastor walked slowly into Marshall's room where I was still staring at the bike. He paused in the center of the room for a second, then went over and placed his hands on the window sill, propping his chin on the top sash.

"Ray, sometimes I get so depressed that buying something is the only way to keep my senses," he said in an apologetic tone. "I know God will supply our needs, but sometimes it's hard to wait on His timing." There was another moment of silence as Pastor stared out the window. "If it's repossessed, at least I'll have had the enjoyment for a little while."

"Ray! Brother Miller!" Buck yelled up the basement stairway.

"Up here," I yelled back.

Buck pulled himself up the stairs with the handrail and puffed into Marshall's bedroom. His dirty T-shirt was wet in front, and sweat dripped off his forehead onto the floor. "Are you two going to stand around the rest of the afternoon and stare out the window? The trucks are loaded, and Hank said to tell you after this load he's calling it a day. Let's go!"

"OK, soon as I get this window shade fixed we'll be right down."

Buck never noticed what we had been looking at, so I never mentioned it. Neither did Pastor Miller. The blind stayed so I followed them down the steps. "Man I wish I had a swimming pool to go jump into. It must be 100 degrees out there."

CHAPTER FOUR

THE DOUBT

Tax problems grew more desperate for Laity. Work nearly came to a stand-still and I.R.S. agents frequently showed up demanding Form 941 payments to which there was no money left to draw from. The agents could care less about outstanding Accounts Receivable. They wanted payment now, regardless of how I came up with the monies. After several weeks of continuous hassle they put a lean on our van forcing us to relinquish it at a substantial loss.

Just two days after receiving notification, at 7:07 a.m., I watched from my living room window, the repossess-or hook a cable to the Econoline-150 frame, which was parked in front of my house, and hoist it onto a carrier. The passenger west coast mirror caught an upright bar on the carrier, snapping glass into the street. They secured each axle and drove away, not carrying about the glass still scattered in the street. I went out with a broom and dust pan and swept up the glass for fear it would get into my car tires. Thank God I'd thought to take my tools, ladders, loose sensors, other inventory, and repair parts out of the van the night before.

Two weeks later I received a bill from the Ford dealership which showed the balance owed. I said to Bonnie, "They even had the audacity to add the cost of a new mirror! I can't believe they charged me $235 for a new mirror they broke!"

The tenant below our office had expressed interest in our second-floor location nearly a year ago, so I made up my mind to work out a deal with him. Our location had a private glass-door entrance at the top of a spiral staircase, and he really liked our frontage view. He had out-grown his small, first floor, two-room office space which had all four windows blocked by shrubbery which had reached six feet high. He agreed to come up right after lunch.

The deal was settled. I chose a single small desk in a room near the back of the office; he took the reception area, both front offices and the room we had used to house our inventory. After we received the owner's approval, he assumed the balance on my lease to which I paid him $50/month to have an answering machine set on a desk. I sold some office furniture to him and left him have the balance at no charge. I figured I would sell before I.R.S. could take it also. I spent the rest of the day making several trips to and from home, taking files, books, personal items and essentials needed to have my office relocated at home.

I converted Shelly's bedroom into my home office, moved all her furniture and possessions to Richard's room, and all of Richard's furniture and belongings downstairs into the former game room. Richard liked the large room, but my ten-year-old, Shelly, was not at all happy with Richard's room. She did not want a "boys" room with a basketball-in-hoop for a ceiling light, walnut crown molding, red and blue striped wallpaper one third the way down each wall resting on a walnut chair rail, nor bright red carpet.

The first night everyone was too tired to complain, but the second night Shelly came into her former bedroom where her bed used to be. I was sitting at my new desk location trying to organize some paperwork. "Honey, what's wrong?" I asked when I saw the tears in her eyes and glancing at the clock to see how late it had become.

"I don't like sleeping in Richard's room? (Sob) It's a **boy's room**."

"Come here!" I said as I pulled her up onto my lap. "It's only temporary until Daddy figures out what else to do. Stop crying. You'll always be Daddy's little peanut?" This was my nickname for her ever since she began walking.

"What about the baby?"

"Daddy has only **one peanut**, and that's **you**. I love you so very much," I assured her as I hugged her real tight. "Now you go to bed, OK? Daddy'll come in and tuck you in."

"OK!"

She constantly complained about the basketball light each night until Bonnie finally placed a small lamp beside her bed.

With all the tax juggling and the need to first have my corporate returns completed, my personal income taxes fell into arrears as well. On several occasions, within minutes after I left the house to complete simple add-on installations or make a service call, a very belligerent I.R.S. agent, would show up at my home in Woodbridge, and harass Bonnie sometimes to tears.

I tried for a small business loan from several establishments, but to no avail. I even tried asking Gene and Stanley Westriech, the owner of several office buildings in Arlington, for a loan, but both refused. Stanley, a long time business friend, said, "Ray if you or your family needed food or medical service I'd be happy to help you out, but I don't want to invest in Laity."

All hope was fading. I'd go to my "single-desk office" in Springfield each morning to check phone messages, pick up Laity mail, hoping for a few checks, and pray daily for a break through, but it seemed the more I prayed the worst things got. It became more and more difficult to maintain even a single crew, while working out of my house.

One of the saddest things I had encountered was to see Pat, my secretary, leave before closing my office in Springfield. More times than not, she had sensed my grief and depression and would read encouraging promises which she had marked in her Bible, but I stopped believing these promises were meant for me.

Pat was a former expert at analyzing people's hand writing, in addition to her office management skills. Often an FBI agent, and an associate of his, would come in and have her analyze notes or scripts from cases they were trying to solve. By the way people made their letters she could determine mood swings, personality traits, education, gender, and other social traits of individuals. The larger the manuscript, the more definite she would be. She proved to be quite accurate on many occasions.

At one point they came so often and spent so much time in the office with her that I got agitated because they would use her time without offering a dime for her services. It also bothered me that they would not even apologize for taking up so much of her time, even though, according to them, she helped solve several cases. It got to where they would come two to three times a week until I finally had to say, "No more!"

One time during my office boredom, I even had Pat analyze my own writing as well as Pastor Miller's, in search for answers to Laity's dilemma or perhaps to get insight as to what God wanted of me. Often, I didn't want to believe the results she gave me. In fact, it was hard for me to accept that so much could be communicated from a few written lines.

Sales continued to decrease monthly. Gary had taken another sales position and finally Pat informed me that she was going to try a career in real estate. I hated to see her leave, but I could no longer afford to keep her. She was the most efficient secretary I had ever met. I typed her up the best Letter of Recommendation I could come up with and gave it to her when she left.

Laity sized down to a single two-man crew, work permitting, Austin and me. I assisted in getting one of my other installers, Jerry Welburn, who I had laid off, a job at Goddard Space Center. Within a few weeks I was unable to keep Austin employed either. He needed a full-time job in order to keep up with his house payments, so I called Kastle and asked if they could use a well-trained, hard-working installer. Kastle picked him up almost immediately and with very little additional training, promoted him to foreman.

I stayed in Springfield, at my 48-inch desk, late one evening, after all the other tenant's employees had gone home, just to pray and thank God for providing new jobs for my former employees. Before I headed home I jotted a note to remove the answering machine and have all Laity calls routed to my home on the same number. This meant another phone on my desk at home, and explaining to Bonnie to let the answering machine get all calls.

The next afternoon after placing the phone order I had to go on a service call to adjust the parabolic beams on two infrared sensors. The infrared detectors were installed in a former CIA agent's bait shop. I carried on an extensive conversation with the owner's son, who was temporary filling in while dad was out. His son had been extremely interested in security ever since he had been a teenager, and had become acquainted with all the latest sensors on the market, some of which I hadn't seen or heard of yet. My fifteen-minute job turned into nearly three hours. He was convinced that one day he'd be doing this type of work himself, and the more we talked the more captivated I had become with the idea of conceivably selling Laity. Before I left, I set up an appointment to meet with him and his wife the following Monday evening, at 7:00 PM, to discuss this in more detail.

I helped Gary lay stone all day Saturday around the new former parsonage entrance, but the only thing on my mind was selling Laity. My mind was flooded with, how to present it, how to protect, and insure, my monthly clients, what the asking price might be, could this new acquaintance come up with a down payment, how I would train him, is this for real, what will his wife say, etc.

Sunday came and went and I received nothing out of either service. The only thing on my mind was how to unload Laity while still remaining faithful to my 83 accrued monthly clients, who trusted me with monitoring their homes' security systems, and for which I was averaging nearly $1000 per month income.

I completed one local service call in Dale City, at a church member's home by 11:00 o'clock, came back home, made a turkey sandwich, and shuffled papers (mostly bills) the rest of the afternoon. It was great to break from the depressing work, to feed and burp Cindy, and spend a little time cooing at her before she dozed off. Soon Shelly and Rich's school bus arrived and I watched from my new office window as they walked down the sidewalk and bid their neighboring friends farewell.

Finally, it neared 6:00 o'clock, so I put on a suit and tie and headed up I-95 to the Springfield exit en route to Wayne's home. I didn't want to be late so I didn't waste any time.

"Lord," I prayed, "I could use your help if you're still listening. Please give me the words as I meet with Wayne and his wife. In Jesus name. Thank you Amen."

Apartment 207 was up one flight of stairs, less than a mile from my former Springfield office. My heart started beating double time as I pressed the lighted doorbell button.

"Ray! Come in," Wayne said. "Vickie will be right out. Let's go in the living room. Can I get you something to drink?"

"No thanks, Wayne. I just finished two cups of coffee."

"Well I'm having an iced tea myself. You sure I can't bring you a glass?"

"OK, if it's no bother."

"Not at all. I live on iced tea."

"Vickie, this is Ray Sines, the man who's company put the security system in Dad's bait shop."

"Please to meet you Mr. Sines."

"Please. Call me Ray. It's a pleasure to meet you too Vickie. I'm sure Wayne has shared that I am interested in selling my company."

"Yes! Some," as she took a seat on the opposite end of the baby blue sofa. Wayne has always been impressed with the latest security technology. Look at that magazine rack. He doesn't miss any."

"Come on Vic. There's new stuff every day," Wayne said defending his magazine library. "I just like staying up with everything. Let's hear what Ray wants to talk about."

I wasn't quite sure where to begin so I started where I had left off when I last talked with Wayne. "I tried to make clear to Wayne the other day; I've lost the enthusiasm I once craved to continue in this career. Don't get me wrong. I still believe in doing the best work possible, but the zeal is not there. So to make a long story short I've decided to offer my company to you and Wayne for $5000 down and $500 dollars per month for five years. I will train Wayne each day and introduce him to all my clients over the next six months during which time Wayne will be learning installation techniques, without pay of course. In addition your payments won't begin until Wayne is fully trained. I'm sure, as well versed in sensors as Wayne is he will be fully trained by then."

"What are you going to do for income during training?" Vickie asked Wayne.

"I'll draw some out of savings, and help Dad during evenings and weekends," Wayne assured Vickie. "And you can help me set up files on Sundays."

"Leave me go on," I said before Vickie could get cold feet. "I already have 83 accounts like your Dad's which I receive $300 per year from each account for monitoring fees. That s a guaranteed income total of $24,900 each year. Plus every few years you can raise the monitoring fee to keep up with the cost of living. In other words, if you never sell another system you'll still have this yearly income plus people are always adding something here and there or changing doors, windows, wanting a different entry code number, etc. All of these changes become billable at whatever hourly rate you set. And, I'm sure we'll sell a system or two while Wayne is being trained."

"What are the downfalls?" Wayne asked making sure he wasn't over looking anything.

"Well, to protect my clients who have put a lot of trust into Laity, I drew up a continuous plan. If you sell the company anytime during the first year I will receive 100 per cent of the sale. If you sell anytime during the second year I would receive 90 per cent of the sale. The third year 80 per cent. The forth year 70 per cent and the fifth year 60 per cent. This guarantees my clients monitoring protection for five years."

"Do I have to keep the name, Laity?" Wayne asked.

"Not after final payment. No!" I assured him. "You can call it whatever you wish."

CHAPTER FIVE

THE ANSWER

I was in front of Wayne's apartment at exactly nine o'clock. As soon as he saw me he came outside, wearing a pair of blue jeans and a bright blue polo shirt with two pens in the shirt pocket, a small spiral note pad in his right hip pocket, and a small brown lunch bag in his left hand. I was impressed already.

"Morning Ray."

"Morning Wayne. You ready for school to begin?"

"I sure am. Talked about it most of the night. In fact, Vic's getting a cashier's check drawn up today."

"That's great," I said "because I got an order this morning for a code change, right after I show you the computer-printer set-up. I told Mrs. Deter we would be there before lunch."

"Did she say why she wanted her entry code changed?"

"Yes, she let her temporary maid go and she didn't feel secure with her knowing the old code. This happens a lot, especially people with new money."

"What do you mean 'new money'?"

"That's what we call people who are not born into families with money. They've just recently made it big. They're always the hardest to work for. Sometimes it seems impossible to please them."

"Sounds like working for my Dad."

"Wayne you'll find there are others who you'll love working in their homes or businesses. They respect your professionalism as you learn to respect theirs."

"I have a lot to learn, but I'm eager to learn."

"Just be totally honest and up front with everybody." I said to Wayne. "Most of my clients have become good friends. I trust they will become yours as well."

We spent a couple hours going over the computer/printer capabilities at the monitoring center, and then afterwards I called two clients who voluntarily set off an emergency alarm test and a burglar alarm test at their homes so Wayne could see how the incoming codes differed and how an actual alarm is to be handled at the monitoring center. He took several pages of notes and asked several questions.

"Well Wayne, we need to get on the Beltway to Potomac, Maryland and change Mrs. Deter's entry code at three doors. It's already going on 11:30."

"How do you change an entry code?" Wayne asked.

"First, we have to go to the main control panel and temporary disarm the tamper switches behind the keyless entry units. Then we'll individually reprogram each unit's minicomputer. I'll show you on the first one, and then I'll watch as you reprogram the other two. Everything will be on-the-job training. By the time six months are up you'll be a pro."

"This is exciting. I've taken several electronic courses, now I finally get to put them to use. This is like a dream coming true."

The $5000 cashier's check helped tremendously and allowed me to clear up several past due tax debts. At least I. R. S. wasn't sending an agent every Monday as before. Although I continued to get phone calls to which I didn't have the answers they were looking for.

I've always enjoyed training eager technicians. Wayne learned quickly. I actually looked forward each morning to being in the field again, and I very much enjoyed teaching a willing apprentice. I prayed each night for God's help and for continued revenue.

Spiritually I neared my breaking point. In fact, one night before going to bed, I knelt at the living room sofa and insisted, "Lord, if you want me to preach then have someone come and look me straight in the face and tell me, 'Ray God has called you to preach.' Otherwise I'm going to do what's best for my family and I'll not pray about this again unless you answer verbatim. I'm tired of trying to second guess you! So, it's totally in your hands. Amen!"

Pastor Miller had accepted the Virginia State Youth Director's appointment about a year and a half ago, and our State Overseer, The Reverend Charles Conn, assigned us, Reverend

Gary Carruthers from Winchester, Virginia. Pastor Carruthers was a great preacher, but he was not Brother Miller. I really felt bad that he got stuck, having to raise funds to pay all the church bills that had accumulated from our building program.

Over the next two weeks Wayne and I had finished a new installation in a Georgetown townhouse. During this time period, Wayne had purchased a complete set of installer's tools, equipped his Eagle with bins and racks to hold small hardware, and purchased several additional kinds of window sensors along with a few seismic sensors that looked quite attractive. The older seismic detectors would often false alarm during thunder storms, but Wayne insisted that the sensitivity of these new units are filtered at the control unit, before being fed into the burglary loop. I slowly gave in and let him make these types of decisions, knowing it would soon become his call, totally. Each day I worked to further his confidence in service, installation, and in determining what type of sensor(s) was best suited for each covered area. Wayne's biggest problem was fishing wires inside walls, but this was a common frustration with all new installers until they had completed several installations with a trainer's help. This was something that couldn't be pushed. It had to be experienced firsthand until the installer's confidence was built up.

That Friday night Brother Miller called from Roanoke to inform me that he would be in Dale City tomorrow and wondered if he could crash at our home for the night, before driving back to Roanoke Sunday morning. "Certainly," I said. "Rich can use the sleeping bag and you can use his bed. What time will you be getting in?"

"Around eight o'clock tomorrow evening, if that's ok?"

"Absolutely, no problem. I'll be here."

"OK! I'll see you then. You're sure it'll be ok with Bonnie?"

"Yes, she's standing right here beside me in the kitchen. See you tomorrow evening. We'll catch up on old times. See ya then."

"Now what's Brother Miller want?" Bonnie asked thinking he wanted me to do something with him.

"Nothing! He just needs a place to crash before driving back to Roanoke Sunday."

Brother Miller didn't arrive until nearly 8:30 p.m. We had about ½ hour of daylight left.

"Hello Brother! Come in. Hope you're hungry cause I ordered two large sausage and pepperoni pizzas that should be arriving any minute."

"I'm famished. Thanks. I wasn't able to leave as soon as I wanted to, and I've been driving for a little over four hours."

"Here, let me take your suitcase. Come on down to the dining room and get some Diet Coke. The pizza man should be soon."

"How are you and little Cindy doing Bonnie?"

About that time Cindy slid down the upper steps and peered through the open wrought-iron railing. Bonnie saw her, as she come out of the kitchen.

"See she's not so little any more. She already tries to boss the entire house; and gets into everything. She really keeps me going."

"Time sure flies don't it?" Brother Miller said turning around and patting Cindy's hand through the railing.

"Yes. Can you believe she'll be two in three weeks?"

"So, what brings you up our way?" I asked. "Has the church in Fairfax sold yet?"

"No, nothing with that. I needed to visit some people. You probably know Sister Fair isn't doing well. And Urple isn't taking it well."

"I haven't seen Urple since she started going to church in Stafford, and I don't visit much anymore because I stay extremely busy training the buyer for Laity."

"Who's buying Laity?"

"Wayne Harper is in the process, but he's got a ways to go."

Ding dong!

"Pizza's here! Rich! Shelly! Cindy! Come on! Let's eat while it's hot!"

We killed the two pizzas and the kids went upstairs to watch TV. Bonnie was cleaning in the kitchen while Brother Miller and I remained at the dining room table talking about Laity, the church and several people we both know well. I had told him that Austin, our church clerk, was now working for Kastle Systems and doing really well. Time flew by. Bonnie and the kids had gone to bed an hour earlier and were now asleep. It was already after midnight. We continued to chat in between my yawning. "It's going on two o'clock in the morning Brother. My eyes won't stay open any longer I got to go to bed," I said rubbing my eyes and yawning again. "Your bed's in the former game room, now Rich's bedroom."

"Ray, I have to tell you something before you go upstairs."

"Well say it Brother."

"I was in my office praying yesterday morning about eight o'clock and God spoke to me and told me to come here, look you straight in the eyes and tell you *'He has called you to preach.'* He wouldn't let me rest until I told you."

The very moment Pastor Miller said, *"God has called you to preach,"* my hands and arms went up in the air and I started weeping and praising God. The Holy Spirit came upon me and I began speaking in tongues, continuing to praise the Lord. I'm not sure how long I stood there praising God, but finally I gathered my composure and bid Pastor Miller good night and thanked him for his obedience to God. I felt a peace come over me that I hadn't experienced in a long while. I turned out the lights and went upstairs. I made it as far as the living room sofa. Still overwhelmed with God's answer, I knelt down at the same spot in front of the sofa, wept, prayed, rejoiced, and thanked God again and again. It was three in the morning when I finally got up to go to bed.

I no sooner sat on the edge of the bed to pull off my socks, when Bonnie yelled, "You can't have her!"

"Bonnie!" I said trying to shake her awake. She pushed toward me so forcibly that I went backwards. I shook her again, "Bonnie!" This time she rose up forcing me away with strength I knew she didn't own, screaming clearly.

"You can't have her!" she shouted.

At that moment the Holy Spirit came upon me, and I took hold of Bonnie's shoulders and prayed with the force of God, "Devil, I command you in the name of Jesus Christ of Nazareth, leave my wife alone! Get out of my house and stay out! In Jesus' name!" I no sooner prayed when Satan literally appeared, dressed in a dark black pin-striped suit, giving me a skirmish smile as he slowly excited the open bedroom doorway, staring at me as he left. Bonnie fell back from her sitting position onto the bed like a wet dish cloth.

"Bonnie!" I shouted again. This time she threw both arms around me and held me so tight I could hardly breathe. "Are you ok?" I asked.

"I was having the most awful dream! It was so real. Satan had my Mom dragging her down a black whirlpool. I had hold of her hand, but he was pulling her under. Every time I pulled her head up, he yanked down." She said trembling.

"It's going to be alright!" I assured her. "God will help you."

"Ray, I don't want Mom to go to Hell." She cried, wanting assurance her Mom would be ok.

I never told her, at that time, whom I had seen leave the bedroom after I prayed, but I did assure her again that God had everything under control. I quoted her the Scripture text, *"Greater is he that is in you than he that is in the world"* (1 John

4:4 KJV). I held her tight until she went back to sleep, praying and thanking God the whole time.

A few hours later, at breakfast, I asked Brother Miller if he heard us last night.

"No!" He said, "I died after you went to bed until my alarm went off this morning."

I shared with Pastor Miller what happened after he had gone to bed. Bonnie was out of hearing range and I didn't feel it was the right time yet to share anything about me being called to preach. We finished eating and had gotten ready for church as Brother Miller headed out the door, back to Roanoke. I had such peace knowing for sure what God wanted me to do that I could hardly contain it. I made up my mind, Lord willing, to tell Bonnie everything after lunch today.

I was still on a spiritual high, as we joined several other church folks at the Chesapeake Bay Seafood House, even though I couldn't remember one thing from Pastor Carruthers' sermon. I ordered crab legs (the most expensive item on the menu) because that entitled me to seconds of anything else on the menu. Many of us followed this same format because it was all you could eat.

We stuffed ourselves and bid our farewells. Normally I'd go home afterwards and take my Sunday nap on the sofa because evening service always began sharply at six o'clock following 30 minutes of choir practice. Today, when we got home, I took off my Sunday clothes, put on jeans and a T-shirt and sat on the bed. Without hesitating any longer, I called for Bonnie and all three children to come here a moment. Richard had a *'what did I do now?'* look on his face as he entered the bedroom. Cindy ran and jumped up on the bed. Shelly came through the door slowly followed by Bonnie, who had gone to the kitchen to put some left-over's in the fridge.

"Now what?" Bonnie asked expecting something had happened.

"I need to talk to you all as a family," I began. "God has called me to go into the ministry and I have accepted His call."

"What do you mean go into the ministry?" Richard asked.

"I mean God has called me to preach," I responded. "And I waited to tell you all at the same time."

"Does that mean we'll have to move?" Shelly asked.

"Maybe, I don't know yet, but whatever it means, we will do it as a family."

Then Bonnie burst out in anger, "There's no way I'll **EVER** be a preacher's wife! What did you let **BROTHER** Miller talk you into now? I knew he had something up his sleeve!"

"Bonnie it's not that way at all. I had prayed several weeks ago and asked God 'if He wanted me to preach, then He had to send someone to look me in the face and say, God has called you to preach.' Brother Miller was just obeying God."

My response made Bonnie even more furious as she continued, now very loudly, "God may have called **YOU,** but He didn't call me! And the next time I see Brother Miller I have three questions that I demand answered from him." She grabbed a change of clothing and stormed into the upstairs bath slamming the door behind her.

The kids and I remained on the bed with Cindy now on my lap and my other arm around Shelly. She and Rich wondered about school, their friends, where we might live, how I would know where to go, and other questions that children who never experienced Mom and Dad fighting in a long time might ask. Unfortunately most of their questions I couldn't answer, but I assured them that God knew what He was doing and that He would take care of everything in His time. I hugged them real tight and told them how much I loved each of them, and that God would give Mommy understanding too. Needless to say, no one got a nap this afternoon.

I went to church alone that night, needing a whole lot more encouragement from God. The hardest thing for me was answering all the, "Where's Bonnie?" questions. I simply said "she wasn't feeling well" and left it at that.

The next morning I went to work as usual, meeting Wayne and riding with him to the job. That morning his classical music, which he played loudly every day, really got on my nerves. I begged for the first time, "Could you please turn that down?"

"I'm sorry. This clears my head."

"Not mine," I responded. "It gives me a headache."

At that Wayne cut it to half volume. Everyday got harder to concentrate on Laity, but today I was especially frustrated.

I had half a mind to tell him I wasn't feeling well and would probably have to go home early.

Bonnie had fed Cindy breakfast, placed the dishes in the dishwasher and was cleaning up the table when the phone rang. She picked it up in the kitchen because the cord reached all the way into the dining room.

"Hello."

"Sister Sines," Brother Miller said, to which Bonnie jumped in quickly.

"Ray's not here! He's at work!"

"Actually I didn't call to talk to Ray. I called to talk to you," Brother Miller continued before Bonnie could speak again. "Your answer to question number one . . . question number two . . . and question number three . . ." The phone fell out of Bonnie's hand and bounced off the counter onto the floor. "Sister Sines," Brother Miller shouted. "You ok?"

"I'm sorry, Brother. The phone slipped out of my hand." She then apologized and asked Pastor Miller how he knew . . .

"Bonnie, the Lord told me to call and give you these three answers the same as He told me to come and talk face to face with Ray. I know this is hard for you, but God will make everything clear in time."

"Thank you Pastor Miller," she said apologetically as she was about to hang up the phone.

"Remember, I'm only a phone call away. If you need anything call me."

"Ok. Bye."

That night, in a much calmer tone than the previous night, Bonnie told me about her call from Pastor Miller, yet she refused to tell me what the three questions or answers were. I didn't push it. I figured she'd tell me in her own time. I didn't really care.

"There's no way Brother Miller could have known that," Bonnie confessed, "Boy I sure have a lot to learn about God."

"Don't we all?" I assured her.

I wasted no time finding how to go about getting into the ministry, I called Pastor Stone, our District Overseer, and he informed me that General Headquarters had recently developed a new Ministerial Intern Program called the M.I.P, but it requires leaving your church to study under another pastor for seven consecutive months. In fact, he said, the first class is scheduled to begin in two weeks; if I hurried I could pick up the forms at his office, mail them in along with the $130 entrance fee, and I could get enrolled just in time. My family and I were required to attend every service (three times per week) at the sponsoring church. Also, during this time both Bonnie and I each were required to read the Bible completely through along with 33 other assigned books during the seven-month period. The "Master Pastor" would be responsible for keeping us on track with our daily reading, and monitor our daily physical exercise program, which we were to adhere to Monday through Saturday. In addition, we were required to accept and perform teaching assignments, at least once, in each class, and I had to preach at least three sermons in their church either Sunday morning or Sunday night as well as teach the Adult Bible Study twice on Wednesday night.

Brother Stone made it sound overwhelming, but I made up my mind to give it a go. In addition, we had to drive to Roanoke one weekend per month, be tested on our scheduled reading assignments, and listen to lectures given by several scheduled ordained ministers who included our State Overseer, The Reverend Charles Conn. I was required to maintain a minimum 70 percentile. Bonnie had to test each month too, but no records were retained of her scores. The morning tests were on Scriptures only, while the afternoon tests were taken from our text book assignments.

The following morning I got the ball rolling by filling out our applications. I had Brother Stone sign-off on them before I left his office, wrote out a check to Church of God State Headquarters, and dropped everything off at the Post Office. According to Pastor Stone, our notebooks and first set of assigned text books would arrive in about a week from Roanoke. He had our first trip to Roanoke scheduled for Friday, October the 13th.

Bonnie and I started reading four chapters from the Book of Genesis and two chapters in Matthew that very evening. Even though she didn't want to do the reading, she didn't want to get behind even more. Since we were required to read a total of six chapters per day, six days per week, we agreed to both get a head start on our Bible reading even if we didn't have the text books yet.

CHAPTER SIX

THE WAIT

I was excited to come home from work and find UPS had delivered our books. I couldn't wait to tear the package open. Bonnie and I were already seven days ahead in our Bible readings, and now with two days left to begin our book readings we could both get a head start on <u>Partners in Ministry</u> by Dr. James L. Garlow. The subscript on the front of the book grabbed my attention: *Laity and Pastors Working Together.* The word *Laity* reminded me I was finally on the right track. I perused through the 3-ring binder containing our reading schedule, exercise logs, amount of time spent in prayer each day, along with the other activities we were to accomplish at our Master Pastor's church in Alexander, Virginia. I felt like a kid on Christmas morning, eager for dinner to be over so I could begin reading.

Wayne & I began a small office building installation today which I figured would take a full week to complete. He was excited, but new installations ceased to hold my attention like they had in the past. However, for Wayne's sake, I put on a good front for him and his new customer. I was happy to see him excited, especially since he had a big part in landing the new contract.

Weeks crept by slowly at work. Wayne was getting the hang of installations. We celebrated with his iced tea and my Diet Coke after he successfully snaked a wire up through his first wall, solo. I gave him a high-five and took a fifteen minute break to enjoy the moment with him.

Time flew by with our studies. I wondered if it was even possible to have the reading completed before our first trip to Roanoke. From the first nervous Sunday morning, Pastor Weber (our new Master Pastor) and his wife respected our workload. We were honored to be among the first Intern Class ever to enroll in the new Ministerial Intern Program (MIP) and Pastor Weber insisted that he would do his best as our Master Pastor. In fact, the very first Sunday, he took me down to the boiler room and showed me the heating system, the fire and burglar alarm control panels, and the water heater, while explaining that a pastor needed to know how everything in the church worked, which included the mechanical system.

Sister Weber, in the meantime, toured Bonnie and the children through all the Sunday school rooms, bath rooms, and children's church areas. She made Rich, Shelly and Cindy feel welcome treating them as she probably had treated her own children.

"The first couple weeks I'm sure Pastor won't expect too much from you," she said to Bonnie. "We already talked about your schedule and I know he wants both of you to feel at home."

After thirty minutes, we said our goodbyes in the parking lot, looking forward to tonight's service at 6:30. This was our first time going to lunch on Sunday by ourselves in more than three years, so we decided to go to El Mariachi's, a Mexican restaurant in Arlington, where I had eaten many Thursday evenings at staff meetings with Kastle. The Mexican guitarist, who came to our table playing, impressed Rich and Shelly, but Cindy could care less. She was having fun nibbling chips and sipping cool-aid from her sipping cup.

After getting home from church that evening, Bonnie and I, each, continued to read until midnight, even though neither of us had reading assignments on Sundays. Still, we didn't want to get behind either. We wanted to stay ahead of schedule, but liked reviewing together. The month sped by like the Amtrak.

"I can't believe we're already heading to Roanoke," I said to Bonnie as I backed out of the driveway.

"I know," Bonnie responded, "and I'm already feeling a bit query."

Our first Scripture test, Friday morning, was really tough. It included Genesis through Numbers chapter 27 in the Old Testament and Matthew through Luke, chapter 4, in the New. There were 40 multiple-choice questions, 20 fill-in-the-blank questions, and five essay questions. I was amazed at some of the trivial questions which included family members' names, ages, item locations in the Tabernacle, and people in the lineage of Jesus. I had to guess at some answers. Our test results were promised early Saturday morning.

After lunch we took the test on our assigned textbooks. This included anything in our first five books. It was all multiple choices except for five fill-in-the-blank questions. We had two hours to complete it, and then each couple had to tell about their first month's experience at their assigned churches. And of course, let's not forget the talk about exercising. My exercise consisted of working eight to ten hours, five days per week, and walking around our block every Saturday watching Cindy ride her yellow duck. Bonnie's consisted of taking care of the children, cleaning house and also watching Cindy ride her duck down the hill, and over our front sidewalk, with both feet off the pedals.

Early Saturday morning we checked out of the Marriot in Roanoke, ate breakfast and were back at the state office by 8:30 a.m. Two intern couples were already there waiting to get in. The other four couples started exiting their vehicles only minutes later. One of the staff members opened the doors and invited us in. The state office had coffee and doughnuts furnished, already on a table in the foyer.

Nine sharp, we were asked into the same room again. The local host pastor opened with prayer and then our corrected tests were handed to each of us. I saw my score on the top and gave a sigh of relief. Bonnie hid her score and looked as if she was about to cry, too embarrassed to show me.

"Your score doesn't count," I whispered. "I'm the one who has to pass."

This didn't comfort her any. She felt like quitting the program until the speaker said almost the same words I had whispered. She relaxed a little, but wouldn't tell me her score until we were on the road home.

"I can't believe I failed," Bonnie blurted out as I pulled onto I-81 North. "I feel I've wasted my time with all that reading."

"You didn't waste your time. God will bring it back to your memory when you need it."

"I needed it yesterday."

"No! You only have to take the tests, not pass them. Anyway, I know you'll do better as time goes on. Wait and see. God will take care of everything."

We arrived in Dale City just before nine. We had allowed Rich and Shelly to watch Cindy ever since they informed us that our former 16-year-old babysitter had a boyfriend over and spent all her time with him watching TV in the game room. Shelly told her mom and I that she had to do everything for Cindy anyway. So we never asked the babysitter back again.

All three were sitting on the sofa watching TV, alarm activated, so when I opened the front door, setting off the alarm entry warning beeper, Cindy bolted off the sofa and took her normal slide down the top set of stairs, landing at our feet head first.

"Daddy!"

I picked her up, gave her a big hug, pressing in the code to turn off the alarm system before the 20-second warning expired.

Bonnie put Cindy to bed after hugs and kisses as I went out to bring our suitcases in. Shelly was glad to be relieved of her sister for the night. I gave her a big I-love-you hug and kiss and thanked her for being the greatest big sister/babysitter. Rich was more interested in finishing his TV program than all the hugging and kissing.

Bonnie and the older children went to bed around ten, but I felt I needed to read a few chapters in my Bible before retiring.

Each Sunday morning we needed to be out of the house by 7:30 a.m., to make sure we were not late for Sunday school. Rich and Shelly enjoyed their classes, thank God, but Cindy didn't trust the nursery yet, so Bonnie sit her on the pew between us.

After Sunday school dismissed, all the children's classes joined the adults in the sanctuary for Morning Worship. Morning Worship ran 300 plus, with many as seven different cultures in attendance, although the Spanish crowd was so large that they began using the sanctuary at 2:00 p.m. for their own Spanish-speaking service. My dream, for the past five years, at Montclair Tabernacle was to have a multi-cultured congregation like this one.

Pastor Weber, being very mission-minded, had the church send money monthly to build a new church in Trinidad; which was scheduled for completion near the time our MIP internship would end. This Sunday Brother Weber asked me to come to the podium and open morning service with prayer. I had been the Sunday School Superintendent at Montclair so I was at ease taking prayer requests and leading in prayer.

God's anointing on Pastor's message was so strong that his every word pierced my heart. I forgot about Laity, financial woes, taxes, and became so absorbed in his message that I had even forgotten I was on stage. Thirty-five minutes later Pastor gave an altar call. He had everyone in the sanctuary stand, raise their hands, and worship the Lord, while inviting all who needed individual prayer for healing to come down front and stand. He then instructed me to anoint each with oil and pray for them.

The Holy Spirit's presence caused several people to be slain in the spirit as I anointed and prayed for them. God was using me in a way I had not experienced before. I had seen this happen in my hometown church, but now God was using me. I kept thinking, "God I'm not worthy," but He kept using me, no matter how much I tried backing away.

After the service, I stood beside the Pastor at the back door, shaking hands and listening to several comments on the wonderful service. I shook hands with the head usher, and he jumped back, like a bolt of electricity had pierced him in the back.

"You're on fire this morning," he said as if I had anything to do with what happened.

"God is great. Isn't He?" I answered, not knowing for sure how to answer him. I knew I hadn't done a thing, nor did I deserve any praise. I couldn't help but wonder why God would use me the way He did. A lot of things raced through my mind, but I didn't fully comprehend any of them.

Several people gave testimonies of salvation, healing, and being filled with the Holy Spirit in Sunday night's service. I was in awe at the way God had moved. I couldn't help but wonder how God might use me in the future.

The next Sunday I was scheduled to teach the Teen Class and Bonnie, the Kindergarten Class. We both appreciated Brother and Sister Weber so much. Bonnie often commented how easy it was to talk to Sister Weber. She wished she could have talked to her Mom that same way. Pastor Weber respected me as if I had already been a pastor myself. A thought popped into my head of what Derry Edwards once told me, when I had accepted the position of Sunday School Superintendent four years earlier.

"Ray," Derry said, "being a member is like looking at the face of a watch. You look at it all you want, see the time, and enjoy its beauty, but as a Superintendent you take the back off, look at the gears and blow the dust out when needed."

Talking with Pastor Weber made me feel as if I was preparing to work on the gears and oil them as needed. He had been an Overseer on the mission field for several years, training and counseling new church pastors who had come up through the ranks as elders, who had later received the call into the ministry. He had physically and spiritually helped to build several churches in Trinidad, Tobago, and even one in Haiti. I felt fortunate to have him as my Master Pastor. On occasion he would even use his learned Trinidadian accent answering, "Yes man!" But when it came to our studies, he and Sister Weber kept us on schedule with our reading; making sure we took time to exercise. Brother Weber claimed exercise put more oxygen in our brains so we could comprehend more.

I lost interest with Laity. Weekly, I gave Wayne more and more responsibility, reminding him that he and Vickie would soon be making all decisions. I worked on building his confidence more than all else. Several times he would ask, "What would you do Ray?"

To which I often answered, "No Wayne. What do you want to do?" Of course, if his answer was flawed, I would explain why it couldn't work that way. He would argue, but he submitted after receiving proof of why he was wrong.

Months continued to fly. It seemed like I'd no sooner got back from Roanoke, and I was re-packing the car for another trip down Interstate 81. I had already received two speeding tickets which forced me to keep my foot off the gas pedal, and fully depend on the cruise control. This soon became the most boring stretch of highway in Virginia, and I complained every time. Bonnie was more content this time because the last two trips she had scored consecutively higher on each set of tests.

I had fallen behind in my reading this time, due to the fact that I spent a week in Boston installing an alarm system in Gene's mother's home. I needed the money so I told Wayne I needed to take a week off from Laity to help a friend with a desperate need. I took my son, Richard and Scott Ryman, a boy Rich knew from Trinity Temple Academy, where they attended private school, to run wires and do the manual labor and cleanup. Gene had purchased all the materials, paid our travel expenses and made arrangements for his mother to put us up at her home. In addition, he volunteered to pay my hourly wage, and the boys wages that I offered them.

We worked five ten-hour days putting sensors on all the doors and windows in her Cape Cod home on Beacon Hill, which had been built in the late 1800s. After we finished, Mrs. Samburgh treated us all with two three-pound lobsters each. We ate at a small Jewish restaurant with a table barely large enough to seat the four of us, but these were the best lobsters we had ever eaten. Like a grandmother, Mrs. Samburgh showed the boys, step by step, how to get every edible bite out of their whole lobsters.

The end of each work day Richard and Scott's routine was to play Risk after dinner, while I read, but I was so tired that the book would often fall onto my face as I dosed off each night. In fact, on several occasions, Rich pulled the book from my face, woke me up from the couch, and told me to go to bed, to which I never objected.

Obviously, my text books' score reflected what book I hadn't read. I guessed at several answers, but the money from

Gene kept us afloat for another full month. Besides, I felt I could live with a "C" on one test. My Scriptures' test was not affected much because I spent a great deal of time reading the Bible, even when I didn't have time for anything else. We had just one more trip to Roanoke, but before this trip, in addition to our regular readings, we were scheduled to visit a small church on our district and two weeks later, a large church. I had already taught the Teen Class, the College Class, and the Adult Sunday School Class, two Wednesday night classes, participated in an Elder's meeting, and preached two Morning Worship services in our assigned church.

The Church of God in Stafford, Virginia, became our small church assignment, even though it had more members than my home church. Pastor Glen Thomas called to confirm our assignment, asking me to be ready to preach Sunday morning.

Sunday school was similar to Montclair, except service began one-half hour earlier. The Adult Class teacher welcomed us, and invited us near the front. When Sunday school was over Brother Thomas invited me to come on stage and sit beside him.

His service opened with a few teens singing, a boy playing lead guitar, and an older gentleman on bass. Brother Thomas' deep baritone voice would probably sound good with any song. I planned to preach one of the same messages I preached in Alexander. Messages were hard for me to put together. I would become so anxious to know the text I felt God wanted me to use, and then, the more comfortable I became with a particular text, I felt uneasy to give my interpretation.

But like Pastor Weber, Brother Thomas asked me to take prayer requests. I listened to several people's requests and then asked everyone to stand for prayer. I began praying for each request I could remember, but then Pastor Thomas stepped up to the podium and began calling specific people, by name, to come up for individual prayer. I stepped off stage, laid my hands on the first person I came to, and prayed the way I had prayed in the past. The Holy Spirit used me as before. At least twelve people were slain in the Spirit, and a few never even made it to the altar. Two in particular went out in the Spirit as they exited their pews, before coming forward, never making it to the altar.

I was amazed as before, knowing I prayed a simple prayer, and the Holy Spirit did the rest. Prayer, again, lasted about thirty minutes. People seemed blessed. Puzzled, I whispered to Pastor Thomas, "Should I preach?"

He said in that same baritone voice, "Looks like the Holy Spirit already preached for you!"

I sought more understanding from the Lord, but He reassured me, He was still in control. We bid our farewells, but Brother Thomas insisted on taking us to lunch.

Over lunch, he and I talked about the time Pastor Miller and I installed the sound system in his church two years ago. Brother Miller and I had spent all Friday night running wires for eight additional microphones which were going to be used for the State Teen Talent contest which was to be held in his church the following day. Most of our time was consumed trying to get rid of an annoying hum, which turned out to be two separate grounds, which caused a feedback loop. Someone, for whatever reason, had grounded the amplifier's metal case.

As soon as I removed the unwanted ground wire, the hum stopped. The sound quality became clean, no matter how loud we cranked it up. It was now nearly seven in the morning. Brother Thomas said, "You guys look like two zombies walking to the van."

The state office had assigned our district overseer's church, Trinity Temple, in Woodbridge, Virginia, as our large church. Brother Stone has been our District Overseer ever since I had my home built in Dale City, and Trinity Temple Academy is where both Richard and Shelly attended private school for the past four years.

I preached the sermon I had intended to preach at Stafford. Services went well, and we were well received, but I didn't feel the liberty I felt in Stafford two weeks earlier. Perhaps I was more nervous due to the fact that Brother Stone was my District Overseer or perhaps because he was less open to the MIP program. We were grateful this was our last MIP requirement before making the final trip to Roanoke.

All the interns, me included, were excited to complete the final tests, as well as all the required readings, and making the boring trips down I-81. The average test scores, we were told, were in the high eighties. It was hard for me to believe that we had actually read 33 books and the entire Bible through in just seven months. At first, I didn't think it would be possible, but as I am learning, with God, *"everything is possible for him who believes"* Mark 9:23 NIV.

The following weekend we needed to drive to Lee University in Cleveland, Tennessee, for graduation, to which, we were invited to bring our families. Graduation was on Saturday at Lee, then the following day we were to attend the North Cleveland Church of God. Fortunately, my youngest brother, Randy and his wife Sherry lived in Cleveland, so we made arrangements to spend the night with them.

Randy and Sherry were proud of us for completing the program, and decided to join us for service at North Cleveland. The "Lee Singers" sang in the morning service, and they sounded awesome. The General Overseer spoke, due to the fact that we were the first MIP graduates ever in the Church of God organization.

We got on the road shortly after lunch to begin the long trip home. Bonnie and I were both to the point of exhaustion, but she refused to sleep, fearing I might doze off while driving.

I had one thing left to accomplish before being authorized to sit for my ministerial license exam. I had to hold a successful one-week revival before becoming qualified in the Church of God for license, even though I had completed the Ministerial Intern Program, scoring a low "A" on my overall studies.

Reverend Jack Thomas, the Pastor of the Boynton Church of God, the church I had attended as a young teen, finding out through my mother that we had completed the MIP, insisted I come and hold revival for him. I kept giving him excuses for weeks why I could not come, but in truth, it was the fact that Scripture repeats in all four gospels, that "a prophet is without honor in his own town." Especially since Jesus said, *"Only in his hometown, among his relatives and in his own house is a prophet without honor"* Mark 6:4 NIV.

I was afraid my first revival might become a failure, but Pastor Thomas kept calling, insisting that his church really needed revival. Finally, I explained my Scripture conviction, but he answered, "Ray, it couldn't get any worse. We only have a handful of people anyway."

So, with this comment, I humbled myself and scheduled revival to begin July 10, thru July 17, 1983. We had made plans to be visit Mom and Bonnie's mother, who lived in the same village, only a fourth of a mile anyway.

Wayne was on his own with Laity, and on June the first, he made his first monthly payment of $500, which was to continue each month for the next five years, until paid in full. This gave me a small income cushion, not knowing what the future held.

I knew the small church in the village of Boynton had no sound system, not that I needed amplification, but since they had no dependable piano player either. I had asked Sister Miller to let me record her playing several songs, for back up if needed. With this in mind, I packed my home stereo amplifier, tape-deck, Fisher speakers; a borrowed microphone from the church, cables needed for hookups, and packed them into the trunk of my Olds 98, in addition to family clothing for a week. Early Friday morning we headed to my mother's because the Sines' reunion, each year, was held there, over the July Fourth weekend.

This year someone counted 97 family and friends in attendance at the reunion. Our family always has a serious time playing volley ball. Sometimes we would have as many as 15 on each team, often with three teams. We played before lunch, after lunch, until everybody was exhausted.

I wondered how many would stay for church. Everyone would have been nice, but I knew that would never happen because several of my family members were involved in their own churches locally. Family members become so familiar with the "old you," it is often hard for them to see you differently. The more I thought about the Sunday morning service the more nervous I became. Thoughts like these flooded my mind all during the reunion, whether I was playing volley ball, throwing horse shoes, or sitting at the table eating. I had only six messages prepared, and no idea what I would say when those were preached.

Around 6:00 a.m. Sunday morning, I went over to the river beside my family home and poured my heart out to God, praying for mercy, power, and guidance. *A prophet has no honor among relatives in his own house,* really made me feel that no one would listen.

"Father, please have mercy," I cried out to God, "in Jesus' name."

I couldn't believe I had allowed Pastor Thomas to talk me into holding a revival in my hometown church. This truly made me depend on God's mercy even more.

I sang the words to one of the songs Sister Miller had recorded for me as if I had done this many times. I don't know if it was the microphone or a different piano sound, but I soon felt the ice break from the piercing stares. I repeated the chorus because that was how I had it recorded for this particular song. Bonnie and I had sung to a few of these same people when we were just teenagers going steady.

After the song I welcomed several family members, a friend of the family who had come to hear me, the church members I recognized, a few from the Meyersdale Church of God whom Pastor Thomas had invited to revival, several children, and three visitors I had never met before.

I began, "My text this morning is taken from Luke 6:46-49 KJV. I titled this sermon, *'The Three Little Pigs Went to Revival'*."

After announcing the title, stares changed to curiosity. People looked at each other, not knowing what was going to come out of this new preacher's mouth.

"Once upon a time there were three little pigs: Perry, Petunia, and Porky. They were getting old enough to get out on their own, and all three had ideas of what they wanted to accomplish. There was a revival going on over in this little village, and a faithful church member called them on the phone."

"Why don't you come to revival tonight?" She asked.

Finally, the three little pigs said, "ok we'll go."

The night they showed up was the last night of revival. They heard the whole message. The preacher preached from Romans 3:23 KJV, *"For all have sinned and come short of the Glory of God."* He continued, "Sin entered the world through one man, and death, through sin, spread to all men, because all have sinned." But, *"if you confess with your mouth, 'Jesus is Lord' and believe in your heart that God raised him from the dead, you will be saved"* Romans 10:9 NIV.

He continued saying, *"For whosoever will call upon the name of the Lord will be saved"* Romans 10:13 KJV.

When the alter call was given, Porky jumped up from his seat and ran to the altar. Petunia saw him go, so she followed him to the altar, too.

Perry sat back and said, "I don't need this stuff, I got a lot of living to do. I got to finish building my house and see the world."

Porky was determined to have an experience with Jesus so he could get into heaven, and his prayer went something like this: "Jesus, I'm sorry for my sins. Will you forgive me? Come into my heart and clean me up. And Jesus, will you give me strength and wisdom to build my future home?"

He really meant what he prayed. Petunia also came to the altar and cried and cried, but she never asked Jesus to come into her heart. She cried because she knew what she had done was bad, but she started thinking about her new house she was building, and all the things she had to finish. Pretty soon she got up from the altar and went back to her seat. Porky seemed to be the last one back from the altar. Finally, he came to his seat, service was dismissed, and they left to go home.

Perry said, "I'm going to take a short cut across the meadow." But he never made it to the other side. What do you think happens? That's right, the raging wolf was hiding in sheep's clothing in the meadow, and roared out and ate the first little pig.

Jesus told us this in the Bible, *"Beware of false prophets which come to you in sheep's clothing, but inwardly they are ravening wolves"* Matthew 7:15 KJV.

Perry never got to build his house or see the world or any of the worldly things he had planned to accomplish. Petunia followed Porky down the road and each went to their own home.

The next several weeks Petunia continued building her house, and she finally was done. Porky, in the mean time kept going to church and praying for Petunia and for wisdom to finish his home.

Every time he saw Petunia he would ask, "Petunia, come on; go to church with me."

But Petunia's reply would always be, "I'm too busy; maybe next Sunday!"

Porky would tell Petunia, "My Bible says: *'Why do you call me, Lord, Lord, and do not do what I say?'"* (Luke 6:46 NIV).

One night storms came and winds blew, and Petunia's house crashed to the ground. Everything she had was wiped out. Her beautiful house and her furniture were both gone. As soon as Porky found out about what happened to Petunia, he searched his Bible to find what the Preacher read last Sunday, *"But the one who hears my words and does not put them into practice is like a man who built a house on the ground without a foundation. The moment the storms came and struck the house it collapsed and its destruction was complete"* Luke 6:49 NIV. Then he went back and read, *"He is like a man building a house, who dug down deep and laid the foundation on rock. When a flood came, the torrent struck that house, but could not shake it, because it was well built"* Luke 6:48 NIV.

Petunia cried out, "Oh Jesus! I'm sorry! I've been so foolish. Would you forgive me of all my sins and come into my heart?"

Petunia felt in her soul that Jesus was saying, "Yes! I stand at the door and knock. If anyone hears my voice and opens the door I will come in . . . ." "For whosoever shall call upon the name of the Lord shall be saved . . ." "He who has the Son has life, and he who does not have the Son of God does not have life."

Amen.

After this simple message, I gave an altar call and asked, "If you would like to do what Porky did, come to the altar this morning, and give your heart to Jesus." There were more at the altar then left in the pews.

Pastor Thomas played his guitar and softly sang a few songs until I had prayed with each person at the altar.

Nearly 50 percent of the Sunday morning attendance came back for the evening service. My oldest brother, Herman gave his heart back to the Lord in this service. I was so humbled when he gave his testimony before the service let out, I couldn't help but cry for joy.

After dismissal he said, "Ray, I need to ask your forgiveness!"

I said, "You don't need my forgiveness. Jesus has already forgiven you."

"No!" He said, "I need your forgiveness for me being mad at you all these years for having Dad's name. I always felt that I should of been named after Dad."

"Herman," I said, "Mom told me that Dad had given me the name Raymond, because when Alberta died, he remarked, 'I had a child die and have never even given any my name.' Mom said that he wished many times he had given you his name, Herman."

I can honestly say that night, Herman and I truly found a love we had never shared before.

Attendance grew each night of revival, and God used simple sermons, with His mercy, to accomplish what He desired to accomplish. Saturday evening, before service, I went back to the river to seek God's guidance again because Pastor Thomas asked me to continue revival for another week, and I didn't know what to do. Because Brother Thomas had informed me that Saturday night we may not have many in attendance I prayed, "Lord, if you fill the church tonight then I'll know you want me to continue another week, if not then I'll close out tomorrow morning."

I went up over the dyke between the home place and the river, but as soon as I reached the top, I felt so guilty for the way I had prayed. I immediately went back down to the river edge and prayed, "Lord, forgive me! If you save one soul tonight, I'll know you want me to continue. Amen."

That night three more souls accepted Jesus Christ as their Lord and Savior. Revival throughout the week had increased in intensity and attendance. On the last night of revival it was 98 degrees, and since there was no air conditioning all the double-windows, in the church sanctuary, were raised as high as they would go. Even both doors in the back were propped wide open.

The church became so full that the Pastor had gathered every folding chair they owned and set them in the middle isle beside each pew. There was still not enough room, so he then had all the children come up and sit on the altar while the special singers, he had invited, remained on stage. A few parents actually had some smaller children sitting on two of the window sills.

After the singing, I came to the podium and saw again, the vision God had shown me, except this time they were real people. I looked out the left sanctuary windows to see an entire family sitting on lawn chairs facing the church. When I turned to the right, I was able to see several people sitting on their front porch, facing the church as well, and I saw one older gentleman sitting on his front porch. In addition to these, I could see people on the left in the parking lot sitting in and on their cars.

In my vision no church walls existed, left, right or in the rear. I could see what looked like no end in sight. It's like people continued from the sanctuary into eternity. The opened windows made the vision more real.

That night God moved mightily in the service. To top it off, one little girl about eight years old was carried up for prayer during altar service. Her left leg had swollen twice the diameter of her right leg. A red line was quite vivid on the swollen leg. When I anointed her leg with oil to pray, the swollen leg was as hot as a stove. I truly believed the Lord had touched her, but I made her father promise me, that if the swelling was still there in the morning, that he would take her into the emergency room. He promised he would.

The girl's father led this same daughter into service during the Sunday Morning Worship service. Her leg was completely healed. In fact, I invited her to come up, take off her pretty shoes, and sit on the altar so the whole congregation could see what God had done for her. Her leg was completely healed.

The next day I went out the street to buy some legal-sized paper from the Justice of the Peace, Merle Baker, to type up a resume'. He invited me into his home while he ripped a new ream of paper open. He said, "We have really enjoyed your revival."

I said, "I never saw you in service."

"Oh no, the wife and I came out on the porch and listened to you each night,"

Silently, I thanked the Lord for the microphone and speakers I had brought with me. As I paid Merle for the paper, I also thanked him for his comment. With Pastor Thomas' insistence, that afternoon, after finishing my resume', I made an appointment to talk with Brother Mark Summers, the Pennsylvania State Overseer. Brother Thomas told me that he had visited the overseer the day after Bonnie and I had our interview with him, and he had told Pastor Thomas that he placed my resume' on the top of his pile for Pastor placements in Pennsylvania.

The next day I headed back to Virginia, knowing God had given me a successful revival which entitled me to sit for my license test at the next scheduled exam date.

CHAPTER 7

THE REVELATION

Satan must really get mad when God uses a mortal to accomplish anything in the supernatural. The very next morning, after getting back to Virginia, an IRS official called, wanting my past two years' 1040 Income Tax Returns. I tried explaining that I was unable to complete them because of uncompleted 941 forms for Laity Enterprises, Inc., and not knowing what to do since IRS had confiscated the company van. He kept insisting that if I didn't file my 1040s, I could lose my home, furniture, and other personal property. Finally, he set up an appointment for the following Monday, 10:00 a.m., at our home to complete the missing tax forms.

We were down to $30 in our checking account, this month's mortgage and the second mortgage a week past due, and now IRS on my back for past due taxes. I could not have imagined getting this depressed in less than a week's time. All I could think about now, was losing our home. My depression, after only a few days, was so severe, in anger, I told Bonnie, "I feel like getting a can of bright red paint, and write in big letters the length of our 24-foot living room wall: '**THOUGH THEY SLAY ME, YET WILL I SERVE HIM.**'" As I headed outside, I said aloud, "God, I'm no Job!"

Bonnie was afraid I would actually do what I said, but after I cooled down, I assured her, "No, but I certainly feel like it!"

We were back at Montclair Tabernacle in the interim, doing whatever we could to help with the ministry. As the service was about to close Sunday morning, a man, I had never met before, stood up and gave a prophecy concerning me.

He prophesied, "I have weighed you on the balance, and you have come to the top. Thus, saith the Lord."

I didn't understand what this prophecy actually meant, but it sounded in my favor so I thanked the Lord, and the gentleman who had obeyed the Lord in giving it. I felt, in the Spirit, it was of God.

Ten o'clock finally came, but the IRS agent became a no show. Finally, he showed up at 10:45. His breath reeked of alcohol. I invited him down to our dining room table, but before he sat down, he asked, "Would you have something cold to drink?"

"I have unsweetened iced tea or ice water," I said. "Which can I get you?"

"Iced-tea please. No sugar!"

I gave him a tall sixteen-ounce glass of tea, and watched him chug down almost every drop without taking a breath.

"Could I have another glass please?" He asked.

"Certainly," I said, removing the pitcher the second time from the refrigerator and refilling his glass. He drank this one nearly as fast as the first. I looked over at Bonnie and she rolled her eyes.

"Could I perhaps have one more?" He asked again.

"Sure," I said as I emptied the pitcher, which I was still holding, into his glass.

"Thank you so much. I was so dehydrated from this heat. Now let me get your 81 tax forms completed for you and your wife to sign."

He did all the writing. I answered his questions the best I could remember. Within minutes we were completed with 1981, and he had us each sign, informing us that we were getting a refund for that year.

"There, that wasn't too hard. Was it?"

"No! Thank God." I answered.

"I don't know about God, but you can thank me."

"Believe me, I am grateful to have it done, and yes, thank you so much." I said, feeling now that God sent this man.

"Now let's get 82 done, so the calls stop."

"You mean I'll be totally caught up?" I asked. "What about Laity taxes?"

"I wrote Laity off! Out of business!" He said. "You'll not receive anything else pertaining to Laity from us, that is, unless you reestablish Laity down the road."

"No, I've learned my lesson there," I said. "I hope I never even see the name again."

Fifteen minutes later, Bonnie and I signed the 1040 Form for 1982, and we were done.

"If you have a copy machine, you can make a copy of these before I take them. Otherwise, I'll mail a copy to this address tomorrow morning." He assured me.

"No, the copy machine was sold too. So if you'd mail them that would be great."

"OK, I'm out of here then."

We each thanked him again, as I closed the front door. Soon as his car left the driveway, Bonnie and I rejoiced and thanked the Lord for sending this IRS Official. It's hard to believe our taxes were done, and we were actually getting a little money back.

I kept anticipating a call from the Pennsylvania State Overseer, Rev. Mark G. Summers, but none came. Six weeks came and went, still no call. Tomorrow, August the twenty-ninth, Richard and Shelly were scheduled to begin their new school year in public schools. I cried out to the Lord Sunday night before going to bed, "Lord, you know Rich and Shelly start high school tomorrow. Lord. I need answers. I can't keep them out of school. I know everything is in your timing Lord, but please give me an answer soon. Amen."

I couldn't understand why God would make us wait, knowing our hearts and all we were going through. I felt like I was just biding time. Richard and Shelly had already completed the second week of school today.

About six p.m. the phone rings.

"Hello," I answered from the kitchen phone because I was helping Bonnie put dinner-dishes in the dishwasher. "Yes Brother Summers. I've been expecting your call."

"Brother Sines, I have a church in Erie. It needs a little work."

"I'll take it," I cut in because I immediately felt the Lord wanted me to.

"I need you there Sunday the eleventh. Can you make it that soon? I did have a minister driving up from West Virginia, but he now tells me the trip is too long and hard on his family and he doesn't want to change his children's schools."

"Yes!" I said. "That gives me a week. I'll take my children out of school, and they can spend some time with their grandmother in Boynton."

"You're District Overseer, Rev. Lincoln Pyle will want you to give him a call when you arrive in Erie. He promised to help the new minister all he could," Overseer Summers said.

"That's great. We're looking forward to coming to Pennsylvania," I assured him.

"I'll give you the phone numbers before I hang up. Also, a Mrs. Lottie Clark has the church key. She lives only a few blocks from the church."

That night Bonnie had a dream, in which she visualized the church sanctuary in every detail. I kept quizzing her because her dream really fascinated me. There was no doubt in either of our minds that God had given her the dream.

"There's one thing that I can't understand," she said.

"What's that?" I asked.

"There was a clock centered above the door on the back wall, and the time on the clock was twenty minutes after eleven. Brother Miller was behind the pulpit. That's when I awoke."

"Dreams don't always make sense," I commented. "If it's from God, it will in time."

The next morning I contacted the mover I knew who attended Brother Stone's church and asked if he could move our furniture? Not only did he agree to move us, but told me that it would not cost me a cent because that was his ministry to other ministers, although, he was backed up for a week. I assured him that would be okay because we planned to have a yard sale tomorrow, and afterwards, I would bring the house and shed keys to him before leaving for Pennsylvania. He agreed.

The next morning our front lawn was filled with file cabinets, desk, chairs, and everything that could be sold, for much needed money to make the move. Our lawn was very visible, so in no time it was filled with people looking for bargains. I refused no offer. I was happy that everything sold so quickly, and that we now had nearly a thousand dollars in cash. The last few items left on the lawn, we had given away.

We dropped all three children off at Mom's on Friday at noon. Mom insisted we eat before driving to Erie. I've never turned down Mom's cooking, so we ate then left for Erie. Three and one-half hours later we exited I-79 onto 26th Street east. The first place I found to get a cup of coffee was on the right, Wagon Wheel eatery, and both of us craved a cup of coffee.

After coffee and a piece of banana cream pie, we continued out 26th Street until we saw the left arrow for Brown Avenue. Our directions said Brown Avenue and 22nd Street, but when we reached the church location I told Bonnie, "This can't be the right church." I was anticipating something far less in appearance, so I continued down Brown Avenue to Liberty Street; made a right on Liberty and another right onto 22nd Street. It brought me back to the same location I had passed the first time.

We parked on 22nd Street, walked up the front steps and peered through the front glass doors. The mahogany paneling in the foyer was exactly as Bonnie explained in her dream. We tried every door, but finding them all locked, we got back into the car and set out to find Lottie Clark's home to pick up the church keys.

Mrs. Clark welcomed us in and introduced us to her 40-year-old son, Bud. She was overwhelmed to meet the new pastor and his wife, and insisted we stay for a piece of cake and coffee. Bud remained in his bedroom, as Bonnie, Sister Clark and I sat at her kitchen table talking over coffee and a piece of bunt cake. She informed us that Bud was not a church-goer. We finished our cake and coffee, received the two keys, and drove back to the church.

When we walked into the sanctuary, it was de ja vu, exactly as Bonnie described it. Of course, the clock on the back wall was the correct time. We left the well-lit sanctuary, walked down the cement steps into the basement, and noticed a lot of unfinished work. The kitchen walls were still the original stone and the ceiling exposed the two-by-twelve joists from the sanctuary floor below the stage. Wires hung from the rafters, and there were only two temporary construction incandescent bulbs for lighting. The men's bathroom had its own problems. The ladies' looked half decent, with two stalls and a 48-inch vanity, and a mirror on the wall above. The fellowship hall had fire-proof, two-by-four foot ceiling tiles with flush-mounted fluorescent lights.

The parsonage is physically attached to the church, so we exited up the rear stairs and opened the door entering the parsonage. I no sooner opened the door when the Lord spoke to my spirit as clear as any human could understand, *"It will not always be this way!"*

Bonnie, walking two steps behind me, when she saw the sight, in disgust, she said, "There's no way I'm living here!"

I knew at that moment, when an overseer says "it needs a little work," beware. The former pastor had purchased his own home outside the city, and envisioned making classrooms where the former parsonage once existed. When the church had run out of money, everything halted and was left in that condition.

There was no bathroom, no kitchen, no plumbing, all rooms but one, had nothing but bare two-by-fours showing on one side, and where the bathroom had once been, it now housed a makeshift PA sound system setting on top of a step ladder with wires hanging everywhere. The ceiling lighting was made up of two eight-foot fluorescent lights strung together. I felt like a missionary in a third-world country must feel as they enter the mission field.

I called Rev. Pyle, explained that I was the new pastor for the Erie Church of God, and asked him if there was any other living facility? He said, "I'm only twenty-five minutes away, Brother Sines, I'll be right there."

Brother Pyle was right on schedule. I had the "kitchen" parsonage door facing 22nd Street, standing wide open to air out the dusty smell, so Brother Pyle came on in.

"Wow!" Lincoln Pyle said. "I knew this hadn't been lived in for several years, but I didn't visualize it like this."

"Where did Lamar and Anna Pirkle live?" I asked. "Did they ever live here?"

"Yes, but only two years. After Anna started working for the phone company, they bought their own home on west 38th Street in Millcreek."

"Brother Summers told me Rev. Pirkle is now evangelizing in New Jersey. Where are Sister Pirkle and the children?"

"They're still on 38th Street. She still plays the piano here when needed. Kevin, their son, still plays his drums on occasion."

"It must have been hard for them to give up the church after nine years."

"Yes. He's stayed here longer than any previous pastor, but the reason I came over was to have you and Bonnie follow me home. Esther insisted you stay with us until this can be made livable."

"We don't want to put you out."

"Nonsense! Our children are all grown and gone, and we would love to have you. In fact, leave this and follow me to North East before it gets dark."

Our drive to North East was the first time I had ever seen acre after acre, with row after row, of Concord grapes. Some areas looked like postcards. Esther and Lincoln reminded me of Mom and Dad. She took Bonnie by the hand and led her to their personal grape orchard. Lincoln and I sat on the deck enjoying the cool evening air, smelling the grapes every time the wind blew our direction.

We were all up before seven. Esther had eggs, pancakes and bacon on the electric griddle frying. "Come to the table while it's hot," she said.

"It smells good," I said.

"It sure does," Bonnie agreed.

"What time are the Sunday services?" I asked Lincoln while we were all eating.

"They've only had the eleven o'clock service for the past three months, and I've been holding Wednesday night Bible study, at seven each week. But I recommend you reestablish three services as soon as possible."

As soon as Sunday's service was dismissed, we drove south to Boynton, to pick up my power tools which I had left at Mom's. We let Mom, Rich, Shelly and Cindy know that we had a lot of work to finish before the family could join us. We left at 6:00 a.m. the next morning so we could work at least eight hours before going back to the Pyle's. Each night, they gave Bonnie and me a lot of encouragement, informing us that they went through similar circumstances in their early ministry.

Lincoln located a toilet that a friend of his had stored overhead in his garage and brought it to Erie for us to install in the parsonage. It was so black, inside and out that Bonnie had me set it out on the sidewalk so she could scrub it and rinse it off with the garden hose. Bonnie had Comet cleanser on a sponge scrubbing inside the tank when an elderly lady walked by and said, "When you clean you really clean don't you?"

We found out the next day. It was Mrs. Reams, our next door neighbor. She was happy to know we were moving in. She thought a lot of Anna Pirkle and told us that she missed her so much when they moved.

The state office had mailed us a $500 check, to help fix up the parsonage. I didn't have the heart to inform Brother Summers that it barely covered the plumbing costs. I Thank God, I took after my father. I could build anything I saw someone else build, if I only had the materials. I had always done my own repairs ever since Bonnie and I were married. I, jokingly, told Bonnie, "Now I know why God sent me here."

The second night back, we had a working toilet. I was grateful not having to go down in the church basement each time nature called. Next, I started plumbing for the vanity, tub and shower.

We both put in fourteen to sixteen hour-work-days. We were so tired after Esther fed us, we helped with dishes, showered, and went straight to bed.

After the bathroom was plumbed, we had to put it on hold until we could afford a tub and vanity.

Next, we divided the large room Rev. Pirkle had planned for Children's Church, into a master bedroom with the smaller room for Cindy. Some building materials were already lying about, but much of it had to be purchased and hauled on top my Olds 98.

The former dining room was becoming Shelly's bedroom, and the blue-paneled room adjacent the master bedroom was going to be Richard's bedroom.

By the end of the second week we felt that we were far enough along to bring the children to their new home in Erie, so we could get them back in school. They would still have to wash up and sponge-bath in the church bathrooms, but it would be like camping out for a while.

All three children had their own first impressions, but we tried explaining it would only be temporary. I drove Richard and Shelly to school the first day, but they realized that they would have to walk a half-mile each way because the city didn't run buses if you lived under a mile from school. We called the mover and requested our furniture be brought out of storage and delivered as soon as possible, but they couldn't make delivery for six more days. So for a week we all had to use sleeping bags. Thank the Lord we had a good microwave and a working refrigerator that had been left.

After I had taken Richard and Shelly to school, I stopped by the local hardware store to pick up some needed items. I had left the side door wide-open, which faced the street, to carry in building materials, when a drunken man staggered in.

"You the new preacher here?" He asked.

"I am. What can I do for you?" I asked.

"I'm headn' home. I just wanted to meet you."

"What's your name?" I asked.

"Raymond. Raymond Rutkowski. What's yours?"

"Ray. Pastor Ray Sines."

"Okay, I just wondered. I'm going now."

I prayed as I watched Raymond stagger down the sidewalk, "Lord. You sent him. Now help sober him up so I can witness to him."

I had just finished Shelly's bedroom when the furniture truck arrived. The movers carried everything in, and placed labeled-boxes where we instructed them. Everything, from my shed in Virginia, I helped carry down the rear church steps into the church "kitchen."

Cindy bounced from box to box climbing on everyone she could. Bonnie and I put the beds together in each of the bedrooms because sleeping bags had gotten old real fast. When Shelly walked in from school her first words were, "How am I going to dress with all these boxes in my room?"

Together, she and I moved her dresser to her desired location, then I opened the box labeled dresser items and said; "It's all yours." She never wanted anyone touching her clothes.

I had put Richard to work in his room, that is, as soon as he stopped complaining about waiting on a "stupid" freight train on their way home Strong Vincent High School.

I asked, "How come you didn't bring any books home again?"

"Dad, everything we're doing, I had last year," he said. "This school is so far behind the schools in Virginia."

I assisted him, as well, moving his dresser into place, and opened the tops of all his boxes; then delegated the rest to him. He figured, as long as the clothes fit and the drawers closed, that was good enough.

We could only receive channels 12, 24 and 35 (the local channels) with rabbit ears, but at least we finally had TV.

Our church attendance had already grown from 12, the first Sunday, to 20 members plus an occasional visitor. It was now late October, with the weather getting colder each week, but I felt we really needed revival. The only minister I knew in Erie was Lincoln Pyle, and I had already counted on him too much as it was, so I called Brother Miller at the State Office in Virginia and asked if he could come and hold us a revival. He agreed to come next Sunday morning and end on Wednesday night.

I finished teaching the Sunday school lesson, took prayer requests, had devotions, and received the Sunday morning offering, but still, Brother Miller hadn't arrived yet. Neither had I prepared anything. I wondered what I would say, as I glanced at the clock on the back wall. It was already nineteen minutes after eleven. I glanced down again to the podium to see if I had forgotten an announcement, and when I looked up, I saw Brother Miller running up the exterior steps into the church foyer.

The clock on the back wall now showed exactly twenty minutes after eleven as Brother Miller opened the sanctuary door. Bonnie's dream was confirmed with the detail that had been missing. Brother Miller had turned West instead of East when he exited I-79.

Revival encouraged Kate McGranner, her two daughters, and one grandson to begin attending services on a regular basis. In addition to them, several visitors attended from the immediate neighborhood, which we met for the first time. Our regular Sunday attendance had grown to twenty-four. As a new pastor, even the growth of six people meant much to me and my family. The only churches my children had known ran more than 100 every Sunday, and most of their friends had attended their church. I felt bad that they had to leave all their upper-middle-class friends to begin life anew with strangers barely above the poverty level.

CHAPTER 8

THE CONFRONTATION

We were blessed to have Brother Miller with us for a few days, but the day after he returned to Virginia we received bad news, also from Virginia. A letter came, with a $1,000 check enclosed from Wayne, informing me that he, under the advice of his lawyer, sold Laity to his wife, and this was payment in full. My old nature wanted to lash out with fury, but after praying and giving much thought about what had happened, God had calmed me down. It took me nearly a week before I gained the right frame of mind, to write a letter to Wayne.

My letter simply stated, "Wayne, you made a legal, business decision, saving yourself $27,500. I'm sure you understand that it will be a great loss to me, but I promised God not to hold a grudge against you or Vickie, so this is a letter of forgiveness. I wish you both the best. Ray."

While driving to the post office, I held the letter up to the Lord and said, "Lord, I'm leaving this in Your hands."

That was the last correspondence between Wayne and me.

The very next week I received a second letter from Virginia, with five yellow change-of-address labels, informing me that our home was going into foreclosure. By the time I received the notice, it was already four days after the foreclosure date, due to the fact that Rev. Pirkle had submitted four separate change-of-address forms for the church mailing address. Since Allstate, my mortgage company, already had a signed contract with a $1000 cash deposit, I had falsely assumed they would handle late payments and fees at settlement. Days later, I found out that it had been the second mortgage company which brought foreclosure, after only two months' delinquency. The second mortgage company assumed our loan, ripping us off of a much needed equity payment of $29,000.

Not that He needed it, but I reminded the Lord, that evening, of His Word where it says, *"I tell you the truth,"* Jesus replied, *"no one who has left home or brothers or sisters or mother or father or children or fields for me and the gospel will fail to receive a hundred times as much in this present age (homes, brothers, sisters, mothers, children and fields—and with them, persecutions) and in the age to come, eternal life"* Mark 10:29-30 NIV.

I prayed, "Lord, I'm certainly receiving my share of persecutions, and I don't need a hundred homes, but You owe me one." I closed my eyes and fell asleep, by faith, knowing He had my back.

Fall quickly turned to winter, and the winds grew colder each night. The curtains on the front windows fluttered with each blast of wind. I placed a candle on the table, for light, one evening after the power had gone out, and we watched the flame change direction each time the wind swirled the snow outside.

The next day I purchased a roll of plastic at Valu Home Center and covered all the windows inside with plastic, held up with many push pins.

The furnace kept going out, so I called Elder Donald Darr, who informed me that the parsonage furnace had formerly been pulled out of another person's home and given to Rev. Pirkle for the church to use. I originally blamed the wind for blowing the pilot out, but Brother Darr said, "It may be the thermocouple."

The pilot went out three more times that same night, so early the next morning I went to West End Hardware, purchased a thermocouple, and installed it immediately when I returned.

I hadn't experienced this much snow since I was a child. Richard went outside, without a coat, to measure the snow depth with a wooden yardstick, and it already measured 22 inches.

"There won't be any school today," he said, brushing snow out of his hair and off his shirt.

But to our surprise, the TV news media reported that schools in Erie City would start one hour late. I allowed Rich and Shelly to stay home, providing he help me shovel and if Shelly would help Mom. They both agreed.

The snow was wet and heavy. Rich and I shoveled for two straight hours, making it only to the church steps out front. We stood on the bottom step to take a break, as it continued to snow at about an inch per hour.

"Don't you hear the Lord calling you to Florida, Dad?" Rich asked wishfully.

"Yeah! Right," throwing snow his direction.

It took another hour and a half to finish shoveling the rest of the steps and sidewalks, but as I walked back to the kitchen door, another two inches had fallen. Later in the afternoon, the sun came from behind the clouds, and where we had re-shoveled was now bare concrete.

Realizing we weren't going to have much of a Christmas, I promised the family I would take them to their grandparents over Christmas vacation. And, Since Christmas came on Sunday, we planned to leave right after church and spend the week in Boynton. Bonnie's parents and Mom lived within walking distance apart.

On Christmas Eve, it began snowing around four in the afternoon and continued all through the night. We woke up to twenty-six inches of snow on the ground. Of course, I had Bonnie call the active church members to inform them that Sunday and Wednesday Church services were cancelled.

Rich and I shoveled from the kitchen door to the car, and cleared the road just enough to get into the car. I started the car to warm it up, while we continued to clear snow from in front and to the rear of the car. Earlier, I had seen a couple four-wheel-drive vehicles on Brown Avenue, so I figured if I could make it to the entrance ramp on I-79; we may be okay to travel south. Rich placed both shovels in the trunk, and we ventured out to see if I-79 was open.

It took thirty minutes to get to the closed ramp, and half way back we got stuck at a traffic light on 26th Street. Thank the Lord. We had the shovels.

As soon as we entered the house, Rich belted out, "79 is closed."

"I wondered what took you so long," Bonnie responded.

So, instead of traveling to Boynton, we played Monopoly until around three in the afternoon. Rich and Shelly each received a single gift from Mom and Dad, which they had opened as soon as they climbed out of bed. Cindy opened her gift from Mom and Dad, and one each from Rich and Shelly.

That night we all watched the traditional, "Miracle on 34th Street," ate pop corn until the local news and the weather forecast was over, then we went to bed hoping to get up early and find I-79 open. We had a little more than enough money for gas and turnpike fares, but I owed this trip to my family.

Mom and Bonnie's parents were happy to see us, and find out how we were doing. They received only few inches of snow on the ground.

I was never so glad to see spring come. It had been a long, snowy, cold winter. And, even though the calendar said spring, we still experienced two additional snow falls totaling more than 16 inches in April alone.

As offerings permitted, I continued to complete the rebuilding inside the parsonage. The hardest physical project was getting a new two-inch, schedule 40, PVC drain pipe to the kitchen sink to replace the now totally clogged steel pipe. Since there was only a six-inch clearance between the kitchen floor joists and the ground, I had to break several cinderblocks out of the wall in the church basement to gain access under the parsonage floor.

Then the work really began. In order to gain access to the sink area, I had to dig, by hand, a ditch, with shovel and hoe, and carry dirt out in five-gallon buckets. After two days digging, I was finally able to military crawl to where the pipe came down through the floor. I hack-sawed the pipe in half, below the floor joists, and then sawed the old pipe into six-foot sections to allow removal. This enabled me to pull the old remaining section up though the kitchen floor, and out through the sink.

After gluing the new PVC traps together under the sink, I measured just enough pipe to clear the joists below, and then I crawled back under the floor to continue the gluing process and installing hangers to maintain a proper drainage slope. With additional PVC fittings, I was able to tie into the cast iron pipe exiting the building, which eliminated all steel piping.

Bonnie was grateful to finally have a working sink in her kitchen again, and not having to carry dishpans of water to do dishes. We even stopped joking about living in "the little house on the prairie."

There were so many unfinished projects, that every extra dime was spent on completing this or that everywhere. With time spent preparing for Sunday morning and Sunday night messages, Wednesday Bible studies, an occasional hospital or home visit, all remaining time was consumed by handyman work.

Each month I became more spiritually drained and discouraged. I would go to bed feeling exhausted, but would lay in bed contemplating every ministry thing I felt I should to be doing as a pastor. Not studying my Bible like I desired hurt me the most. Saturday night after Saturday night, I pleaded through the wee hours of morning, asking God for Sunday morning messages.

Busy work kept me from fasting, praying, visiting, and reading. It didn't take long to realize what a difficult job Rev. Pirkle must have had as well. There were many Monday mornings I felt like leaving too. The only way I dealt with my depression was to continue doing what money allowed to be done.

Later in the summer I found a wood-burning stove I felt would save on gas bills. I hauled it home, cut a section of the living room carpet away in front of the chimney, and built a brick hearth for it to sit on.

We had accumulated a lot of kindling wood from building projects, so to add to this, Rich and I hauled in several small logs to cut up and stored for winter's arrival. We soon had several rows of wood piled up behind the parsonage, and a smaller stack in the church basement.

With winter in mind, we rented an insulation blower from 84 Lumber and purchased ten large bags of cellulose insulation. Rich fed the bags into the hopper outside, while I was in the attic blowing insulation into every outside wall. I came out of the attic looking like I'd come from a coal mine. I was determined to keep the family warmer when the snow came, so I also stuffed paper towels and rags into every crack I could find.

Winter was here again before we realized it, but this winter we felt more comfortable in the front section of the parsonage, although Richard's bedroom and my office in the rear remained cold because we couldn't get into those walls. Nevertheless, it was ten times better than the previous winter.

It was hard to imagine my son graduating from high school this week. It was harder to believe the weather being cold enough in June to build a fire in the stove. About two in the morning, Cindy came to my bedside, as she often did when she wasn't feeling well, and woke me from a sound sleep.

"Daddy, my throat hurts," she spoke right into my ear.

"Wait honey. I'll turn the light on," flipping the switch on the headboard. "What's wrong with this light? I can barely see," I said, nudging Bonnie awake. "Let me turn on the big light, honey."

Cindy's breath reeked from Italian sausage she had eaten the evening before. I snapped on the ceiling light, but it was still so dim I couldn't see.

At that moment Bonnie said, "I smell smoke!"

I had Cindy lay in my bed, while I got up to check the stove draft, thinking someone must have closed it. I took three steps out the bedroom doorway, and fell to the floor. On the floor, I came to my senses, and crawled into the living room with the flashlight I had picked up from the night stand. I saw no smoke coming from the stove, but heard a snapping noise in the wall behind the stove, so I quickly opened the door leading down into the church basement. I spotted fire coming through the wall just above floor level.

As fast as I could crawl, I went into Shelly's bedroom. "Get up! The house is on fire!" Then I raced to Richard's room, woke him and yelled, "Rich, get up! Get some clothes on. The house is on fire. Stay down!"

I pushed the back exterior door wide open to remove some smoke. The breath of cold air revived me enough to race back to the kitchen and open the kitchen door. Now, running, I yelled, "Bonnie, Rich, Shelly, get your clothes on and go out and sit on the church steps. Bonnie, take Cindy's hand!"

Richard pulled out his top dresser drawer and threw it out the back door, and made his way to Shelly's room. She screamed, "You're not touching my clothes!"

"Dad said get the clothes!"

"No Rich," I yelled, "get your clothes on, and go out on the church steps. NOW!"

I watched them all go out the kitchen door, and yelled, "Don't come back in the house for anything. I have to call the fire department!"

I grabbed the phone book, with the flashlight in my mouth, and phone in hand trying to find a phone number for the fire department. I was furious that the number wasn't inside the cover or somewhere easy to find. Finally, I dialed the operator and said, "We have a fire, 928 West 22nd Street! Erie, Pennsylvania." I yelled, "Yes, I'll hold on. Hurry." Finally, someone answered, "Fire department," and I gave the address again.

Remembering the big red fire extinguisher in the church sanctuary, I ran over into the church, yanked the fire extinguisher off the rear wall, and ran back through the rear parsonage door. Quickly opening the door leading to the basement, I pulled the pin from the extinguisher, held the nozzle close to the wall at the fire, and squeezed hard on the trigger. The white powdery contents blasted off the wall into my face, taking my breath away. I fell backward against the crash-bar on the outer metal door, landing on my back, outside, on the sidewalk. The outside air, along with the fall, brought me back to my senses. Using the sleeve of my T-shirt, I wiped the white power from my face, entered through the kitchen door, and ran to the bedroom for shoes and pants because I was still in my underwear.

The fire trucks finally showed up. I told them where I saw the fire, then, I went outside to make sure my family was okay. I ran to the church steps, but they weren't there. I started to panic, when Lucille, the neighbor across the street adjacent the church yelled, "Pastor! They're in my house, on the sofa."

"Bonnie and all three children?" I asked.

"Yes, they're okay,"

"Thank you," I said with a sigh of relief.

I walked back across the street to the parsonage, as two firemen were carrying my stove out through the kitchen door, setting it in the grass between the sidewalk and street. I could only watch from the outside because the firemen wouldn't allow me back inside. Richard saw me standing outside, so he ventured down the sidewalk and stood beside me.

"Did they say what happened?" He asked.

"No. I'm not sure they even know yet," I answered. "I heard one say there was smoke coming out of the sink cabinet."

We both stood there shivering. Finally, Rich asked, "Dad, what's all over your clothes and in your hair?"

I explained the fire extinguisher episode, but he was more worried about me landing on the sidewalk. I never had time to even think about that. I just thanked God for coughing and breathing again.

"I wonder what they're going to cut with a K-12 saw?" I said, seeing firemen hurry through the kitchen door.

In seconds, we heard the saw running. I edged closer to the kitchen door to see into the living room.

"They're cutting a hole in the living room floor!" I said to Rich.

"Why?"

"The fire must have spread under the floor toward the kitchen."

In no time, chunks of floor were being carried out and stacked up against the stove. I couldn't believe how big some of the pieces were. Carpet was still attached to the pieces. Soon they were carrying out six-foot lengths of floor joists, dripping with steaming water.

"Oh, my gosh! They're sawing the kitchen floor too." I said as we both gazed through the doorway.

The charred pile was rapidly growing higher outside. I stepped upon the stoop to peer into the doorway. The fire chief, seeing me, asked, "Are you the pastor?"

"Yes," I answered.

"Do you know if the gas line to the kitchen stove goes across the ceiling?"

"Yes, it does," I said. "The shut-off for the church and parsonage is in the men's bathroom, on the left."

"Yes, we found that, but I wanted to be sure in case we have to cut into the ceiling."

"Do you know what happened yet?" I asked.

"From what we see so far, it looks like the bottom fell out of your chimney, and hot embers from the wood burner landed on the joists. This could have been smoldering for hours." The fire chief commented.

They finally were able to spray the smoldering joists under the front of the parsonage. They busted out several sections of ceiling tile in the living room, and in the kitchen, to be sure there was no fire smoldering in the ceiling insulation. Afterwards, the fire chief told me that we were all very lucky to be alive. He said the smoke level which had reached our beds, and a minute or two later, would have asphyxiated us all and we would all have been killed by carbon monoxide inhalation.

God had used Cindy to spare our lives, without her or us even knowing it. That was the first time I ever thanked God for smelling bad breath. Five o'clock in the morning, after everyone had gone, we stood around the six-by-seven-foot hole in the living room floor, holding each other's hand, and giving thanks to God for saving our lives. It was odd seeing the ground and the ditch I had dug from above the living room and kitchen floors.

Richard asked, "What about my high school graduation tonight?"

"We'll still get there," I assured him. "I'll explain what happened to the principal tonight and work something out so you both can leave school tonight."

At nine in the morning, I called Church Mutual Insurance, and explained what happened. I was concerned about Sunday morning's service, so the claims' department gave me the number to call FireDex, a bonded, 24/7 emergency response company, which the insurance company had used in the past. The claims dept. assured me that they would clean the sanctuary and remove the smoke-smell with an ozone machine.

I made the call to FireDex, in Meadville, as Church Mutual had suggested, gave them the claim number, and the foreman promised to be here within a few hours.

FireDex's foreman showed up with three, two-person crews. Each crew had their own vehicle. They began scrubbing the sanctuary ceiling, walls, windows, doors, wooden pews, and all the church furniture. The foreman installed plastic, isolating the burned area from the rest of the parsonage, and suggested that we use the kitchen door if we needed anything out of the kitchen. We had every door wide open, in which they had placed large fans to remove the burn smell.

After the foreman assured me that they could complete all the work, I signed the contract, giving them the go-ahead to replace floors, ceiling, walls, and anything else they had to do.

"We'll have the sanctuary ready for service this Sunday," the foreman assured me. "But we won't be able to start work in the parsonage until Tuesday."

"That's fine," I said. "I plan to take my family to their grandparents Sunday after church, but I'll be back Monday morning. I'm going to batch here until it's livable again."

"We usually start work at seven. Is that okay?"

"Yes! The earlier, the better for me."

We made it to Richard's graduation, but his cap, gown, and all our clothes reeked of smoke. Everyone showered, and Bonnie had washed the clothes we were wearing, but just walking through the parsonage caused our hair and clean clothing to take on the smoke odor, the same as a smoker bares this hygiene to any nonsmoker. Everyone we passed in the auditorium gave us that look. "We had a fire." I said to a few nearby.

I tried not to let my aggravation affect Richard as he walked down the aisle. Shelly shouted, "Way to go, Rich!"

He graduated with honors, and afterwards, I was able to meet with the principal to explain what had happened. Shelly's teachers agreed to give her grades early, without final tests because they all liked her as a student. Richard was happy to have the pictures over so he could ditch his smelly robe, which couldn't be washed.

Saturday morning I made arrangements to take all our hang-up clothes, bed comforters, blankets, and drapes to Chido's Dry Cleaners on State Street. He agreed to accept our insurance claim number, and to bill Church Mutual directly for payment.

It was amazing that no one from church, had even heard about the fire until they arrived Sunday morning. The sanctuary didn't smell, but the basement did, so we allowed the children's Sunday school class to remain upstairs with the adults. My short message was primarily made up of testimonies from my family and me, thanking God for our lives, being grateful that the fire was contained to the parsonage. I explained what happened to the chimney causing the fire which spread under the floor, and answered questions the best I knew how. Immediately after church, we left for Boynton.

FireDex explained, that due to the sag in the living room floor, they were going to have to replace all the joists and flooring in the living room, kitchen and Shelly's bedroom. I insisted they do whatever they had, to make it right. With this in mind they ordered a large dumpster, to remove all the debris. As soon as it arrived, I helped throw the debris the firemen had placed along the sidewalk into the dumpster. And, since FireDex recommended filling the damaged chimney with stone, so it could never be used again, I placed a "For Sale" sign on the stove, which sold later that afternoon.

Due to the length of the two-by-fourteen-inch joists, half of them were brought through Shelly's bedroom window and the other half were brought through the kitchen window. I enjoyed watching master carpenters at work. My father had been a master builder and I worked with him helping to build my brother Bo's home in Boynton.

In no time these four carpenters had the joists installed and covered with three-fourth-inch thick flooring. It was amazing to see how level the new floor looked, without any more bounce in the middle of the living room. That night, before the foreman left, he handed me a large book of carpet samples to choose from. In the samples I found the exact carpet, color and quality, which we had installed in our living room in Virginia. That was my choice, but the ladies of the church had to approve it.

The ladies were okay with my selection, but two of the elderly ladies felt a chocolate colored short-pile Berber would be better in the kitchen and dining area. They felt it wouldn't show dirt as much. I didn't care for it being that dark, but I lost that battle.

FireDex ordered enough living room carpet to reach Richard's bedroom wall, so it would all be the same color and style. Shipment was scheduled to arrive in about two weeks. I was hoping that everything would be completed before Bonnie and the children came home, but she begged to come home, since she had already been away for two weeks.

As soon as the floor was completed, they removed the old-fashioned kitchen and living room ceilings tiles, the fluorescent eight-foot-long light fixtures, and at my request, replaced the ceiling with drywall. I also insisted they leave out the light fixture on the living room ceiling, and only have one fixture above the table. They agreed without question.

Bonnie was happy to learn that the old 1970s gold, sculptured carpet was being eliminated. In fact, while the dumpster was still out front, I ripped the rest of the carpet up myself, so I wouldn't even have to look at it one more evening.

New, clean painted ceilings and walls, new carpet throughout, and new ceiling light fixtures in the kitchen and dining room, made the parsonage feel quite homey. As we sat on the clean sofa the Lord reminded me what He had said to me when I first entered the door from the church basement into the parsonage. "It will not always look like this," the Lord had told me.

This was beyond comparison to what it had been. We again thanked the Lord for His faithfulness. The total insurance claim ended up being a little over $22,000, of which the church only had to pay the $500 deductible.

Rich and Shelly both found part-time jobs for the summer. Richard wasn't even thinking about college because of our money situation at the church. His Real Entertainment Video job barely paid him enough money for gas in his Chevy Nova which he purchased from my brother, Roger, last winter. Shelly worked at McDonald's, hoping to save enough money for her senior school expenses.

So to encourage Rich, and since I desperately lacked counseling experience, I borrowed $350 from Lucian Tallentire, an elder in our church, to take a fall class in Introductory to Psychology at Penn State Erie, The Behrend College. The college kept the name Behrend because in 1948, Mary Behrend, the widow of Hammermill Paper co-founder, Otto Behrend, donated her 400-acre estate to Penn State for a freshman center. In 1971, Behrend became the first Commonwealth campus to offer four-year degrees. After paying all the enrollment, parking, and student fees, I was scheduled to begin class late that August.

Since I owned the power and hand tools, leftover from Laity, I contracted small building projects and repair jobs at $20 per hour plus materials. After seeing some of the completed projects in the church, my first contracts began with members of the church. Before long, I had worked for nearly every homeowner in the church. Of course, word soon got around, and I had to say no to non emergency work on Saturdays, Sundays, and Wednesday afternoons. I kept those times free for church work only.

I paid Lucian the money I had borrowed in less than 30 days. In a little over another month I had saved up enough money to purchase my Psychology text book at the Penn State book store, and the $480 debt, for the four-credit tuition cost at Admissions office. My school debts were paid two weeks before class began.

Rich began working at Hills Department Store to pick up more hours, still remaining at Real Entertainment one night per week. Both jobs together enabled him to buy much needed tires and the inspection on his Nova. He purchased the state-minimum liability insurance only because he didn't feel his car was worth carrying full coverage insurance on it.

Shelly put $20 per week in savings each week. And, both Shelly and Rich paid the church 10 percent tithes on every dollar, they netted.

I enjoyed my psychology class so much that I enrolled full-time for the spring semester, since the financial aid office informed me that I qualified for a full Pell Grant (paid by the government), a state grant (paid by Pennsylvania Dept. of Ed.), and I was eligible for a student loan, which would cover books, travel, and food expenses.

My finances worked out and this encouraged Rich to apply to, Lee University, our church college in Cleveland, Tennessee. I tried to get him to go to Penn State, but I felt, he needed to be away from home, Erie, and the church "PK" (preachers' kid) syndrome.

Shelly chose to enroll at the Erie Business Center after graduating from Strong Vincent, so I asked, "Why a two-year school?"

"I'm good at balancing my checkbook," she said; "the school is only two blocks from my job, I don't have a car, the school lets out at one p.m., and I can walk to work after school."

"Sounds like you thought this out and already made up your mind."

"Dad, you only have to drop me off at school, and you won't have to pick me up till I'm finished working," she insisted.

"Okay," I agreed feeling her need for independence.

But, interestingly enough, God already had a plan for her car situation. Dennis Queen and his wife, Bonnie, approached me three weeks later after Sunday church. Dennis told me that they wanted to bless Shelly with a car, if I had no objections. "What kind of car?" I asked.

"A 1977 Pontiac Vega Hatchback," he said. "It has high millage, but it runs good. We felt it'd be good transportation for Shelly."

"How much are you asking for it?" I asked.

"No! No," Bonnie insisted. "We want to bless Shelly. We want to give it to her!"

"How can I say no to that?" I said. "But Shelly hasn't even tested for her licenses yet!"

"She'll study hard when you tell her about the car," Bonnie said.

"Thank you both so much!" My Bonnie and I said.

Friday afternoon, before Shelly was to start school, she rode with me up to a new industrial development park in her "new car." I had her parallel park several times, and insisted she use her turn signals each time I said, "Go right or left." After about two hours I told her she was ready to take her test.

The following morning, I let her drive to DMV, while I became her passenger. She was nervous, but I assured her she did well. I watched her drive through the course, only spotting one occasion where I felt she could possibly fail. Finally, she parked the car, opened the door, and came running toward me.

"I passed! Dad, I passed!"

I gave her a big hug and said, "I knew you would, Peanut."

I hadn't called her that in a long while, but her face lit up when I did. I was so proud of her, but I insisted on driving home. I never was a good passenger. I think she spent all Sunday afternoon polishing every inch of her car, inside and out.

CHAPTER 9

THE SHOWDOWN

Before I had taken my first class, I felt it would be hard competing with top high school graduates coming fresh into college. But since my Psychology professor, last semester, ranked each individual's performance with the rest of the class on the top corner of each test, I lost my fear of going full time. Based on the work load in my pastorate, I still felt I should only begin with twelve credit hours my first semester.

After finishing the first full-time semester, I signed up for fifteen credit hours for the spring semester of which, a one-credit hour in Journalism, was spent writing a monthly column titled: *"Let's Talk,"* for the Collegian, our school newspaper. On the Opinion page, my picture was in the upper left corner of the column with, by Pastor Ray Sines, Collegian Staff Writer, centered under the picture. The column enabled students and faculty to recognize me, especially since I spent a lot of study time in the cafeteria between classes with a cup of coffee, studying for my next class.

The Lord used this time and the column to bring students to my table to talk with me. My very first column, based on my first psychology course, was titled: *"What changes your values?"*

In that class I was asked to formulate a personal value list, rated from one to ten, with one being the top priority. Many variables were considered while compiling this list. The overall list varied greatly between individuals, and while many variables listed, appeared on almost every list, they appeared at different locations on the list. This clearly showed the individuality among all the students in the class.

Then, as individuals were put into groups of six students each, the power of peer pressure soon became evident. Individualities appeared to no longer be a priority. Many students changed their values, at least outwardly, after only five minutes of individual group discussions—peer pressures.

Guess what happened when the groups were resolved at the end of the semester? You guessed it! Many students' values changed again—a different peer pressure.

This, one may say, relates to Abraham Maslow's principle on the "lower" levels. The priorities changed because the circumstances changed.

Does this mean in order to change one's value system you have to change one's environment? Yes, to a degree, this will have a direct effect on a person's value system.

For example, if you were sent to prison, for whatever reason, you would soon begin to act like a convict in order to survive in your new environment. On the other hand, if you were to move into a very wealthy neighborhood, you would soon be molded into the "new you" again. So environmental change can make a difference, either positive or negative, and also, this change will have a direct influence on about every aspect in your life.

For example, if you moved into a neighborhood where nearly everyone seemed to get up in the morning to go jogging, you would soon find yourself taking better care of your own body by getting "in shape" yourself—a new peer pressure.

Not including any mind-altering drugs in any form, I believe that, there is only one stronger influence on an individual's value system than that of peer pressure. This powerful influence is a spiritual influence.

This spiritual influence may also be positive or negative— God or Satan, respectively. I speak on the positive only.

I can go along with Abraham Maslow to a point, but I do not believe that a person in his or her own power can become "self-actualized." I do believe, however, that it is possible to become God-actualized.

About fourteen years ago I had set out to climb Maslow's 'pyramid.' My only goal in mind was to become a millionaire. And, perhaps, I was well on my way. I became the vice-president of engineering for a large reputable firm in Arlington, Virginia, with a most excellent salary, expense account, company car, and many other perks and benefits. Ten years later, I became the president of my own corporation. Now, I am an ordained minister. What happened? Did I change my values? Did I move?

Yes, and no. My value system had changed, but not totally of my power. God caused this change to take place in my life.

Yes, I eventually changed my environment because of my new profession, but not vise-versa. My value system had changed because of God's positive influence on my life. God had moved into position number one (with my total acceptance of course). This caused a shift in the balance of my value's list. My pyramid began to take shape downward rather than upward.

The environment is still very important. Certain peer pressures still have certain influences, but my highest priority is now fixed. This number one value priority influences every position below. The bottom values continue to juggle around as life progresses, and perhaps will never settle in a permanent position until death. Regardless, God holds the number one position which determines my values.

Beginning the day of publication of the above first article, students wanted to talk with me, often with the paper still in their book bag. I knew God's anointing was on the column from that day onward. I led more students to the Lord during my first semester than I had to date in my church. This "great commission" continued all through my remaining semesters.

One of my poetry instructors, John Coleman, asked me one day, "Ray, how did you know it was God calling you?"

First, I shared my vision with Mr. Coleman. Then briefly, I explained my former position and goals with Kastle which led to various steps of faith into the ministry. He told me that he was seriously considering going to a seminary, but wanted to be sure it was God's leading.

I said, "John, the Bible says that it is impossible to please God without faith. Yes, it's scary, but you have already landed this position at Penn State, so you can always resort back to teaching. The best that can happen is that you'll know for sure. It's God."

"Thanks. I needed to hear that."

"Do not be afraid. God will be with you."

For the past fifteen years John Coleman has been the Senior Pastor at Abiding Hope Lutheran Church, in Erie, Pennsylvania, and has completed a major transformation with the new building design.

Another example is Professor Stafford, my Physical Science teacher. To me, Professor Stafford falls into the same category as John Coleman because the Bible says, *"Lead out those who have eyes but are blind, who have ears but are deaf"* Isaiah 43:8 NIV.

He had just finished explaining the "Big Bang" theory, and asked the class of nearly 150 students, if anyone else had a theory they'd like to share on how the Earth began. Of course, I raised my hand.

"Pastor Ray! I thought you might want to say something."

"Yes, but may I use the black board?"

"Sure! Come on up."

On the left end of the blackboard I wrote in very large letters, "**ALPHA**," and on the other end, fifteen feet to the right, I wrote, "**OMEGA**." Then I drew a bold line, using the side of the chalk, connecting "Alpha to Omega." On the line, still using the side of the chalk, I wrote in even bigger letters: "**JESUS**."

I then went on to explain that Jesus said, "I am the Alpha and the Omega, the beginning and the end."

Professor Stafford interrupted, "What about the Big Bang theory, since 97 percent of all scientists now believe in the Big Bang theory?"

I answered, "Well, when God spoke everything into existence, it is very possible that His words could have made a horrendous noise. If we were there to hear it, we may have called it a BIG Bang," because when God spoke on Mt. Sinai, many thought it had thundered."

Nearly every student in the class stood to their feet, and gave a loud applause. Professor Stafford, I sincerely believe, thanked me, as well.

He loved parachute jumping, and on weekends in the summer, he would train new jumpers by strapping the rookie to his back, which he called "piggyback" jump-training.

Week after week, he insisted I jump with him, so finally, I said, "Okay! I'll jump, under one condition."

"What's that?" He asked.

"I take a pair of scissors with me."

"Why in the world would you want scissors?"

"On the way down, I start cutting cords until you say, Jesus is Lord!"

"Pastor, you're one crazy preacher!"

As it turned out, Professor Stafford, two years later resigned from Penn State, and went full-time working with his wife making computerized signs, and I am happy to say he is now sold-out to Jesus Christ.

Even Dean Lilly, our Provost, came and sat with me in the cafeteria. He shared how much he enjoyed my monthly column, and that his father was a Baptist minister. These testimonies, at least for now, confirmed that I was right where God wanted me to be.

Several students, during the years I attended Penn State, would often visit the Erie Church of God. In fact, on Easter Sunday, 1988, I had 26 of the 28 students who attended my weekly Tuesday night Bible study class at Behrend, put on my entire Easter Sunday morning program. They sang, played guitars, gave a trumpet solo and a young man in his junior year, preached the Easter message to my congregation.

These youth encouraged our church youth and a few adults to become more active in church. My daughter Shelly, after one year at Erie Business Center, transferred to Penn State to pursue a K-8, degree in teaching. We shared Spanish classes together, an Arts class, and Professor Stafford's Physical Science class. We enjoyed studying together, especially Spanish. If Shelly missed a Spanish phrase in class, Professor Juan Fernandez would say, "Okay Papa Ray, help her out."

Shelly joined the Alpha Sigma Alpha sorority in her sophomore year, and became very close friends with three of the sisters. All three called me Papa Ray on and off campus. My heart ached for one of the sisters named, Tammy because she had shared how close to death her mother was with uterus cancer. She and her younger brother were all her mother had, so we prayed each day for Tammy's mom. Every time the doctors had given up hope, God restored her again and again, and eventually He healed her completely.

Campus life was precious to me as a minister. I was asked by the Student Services Director to Chair the Campus Ministry Board, to which I gratefully accepted. There was rarely a month that went by without me having to counsel students with suicidal thoughts, but mostly from students who were homesick. In three years I even helped four different students transfer into good Bible colleges because all four felt God's strong calling on their lives.

One girl, named Robin Hovey, was healed through our prayers of an eye disease called Macular Degeneration, where her central vision had become very blurry. After God healed her, she gave testimony of seeing very clearly to our church the following Sunday morning before our worship service. At the end of that semester, Robin, with Campus Ministry's help, transferred from Behrend to Nyack Christian College in upper New York because she too, felt God wanted to use her in the ministry.

Our church numbers climbed into the high sixties on occasion, and through my four years in school, God remained my highest priority, whether on campus or in church. It was difficult to complete a BA in English in four years, and maintain my full-time pastorate, but God's grace was not only sufficient—His grace, at times, was overwhelming.

All during my last semester in Spanish class, Juan Fernandez offered anyone in his or her third year, the opportunity to go with him and Lupe to Spain for two weeks. I had enough money left over from my student loan to pay my $1500 fare, but we didn't have the money for Bonnie's fare. Bob Friday, a faithful, loving, church member, heard about us wanting to go, and offered to pay Bonnie's way as a graduation present to me. We took Bob up on his offer, applied for, and received our passports. Then we booked passage on the same flight with Juan, Lupe, their ten year-old-daughter, and two students from Behrend, who had signed up for a two-credit Spanish cultural study for their senior year.

I had arranged our return flight from Spain so I only had to miss one Sunday's service. Of course people were more interested in hearing about our trip than what I preached on. After the short service was over, we showed the many post cards we had purchased viewing all the ancient churches we had visited, of which all were Catholic except for one in Seville, in southwest Spain.

I had to tell about the exciting return flight back to New Jersey. Soon after we had arrived in Spain, Portugal had some sort of political difference with Spain which stopped all air traffic over the country of Portugal. Our pilot was forced to fly down through the Strait of Gibraltar, staying in international waters west of Portugal. The huge passenger plane did not have enough fuel to make it to New Jersey, so we had to make an emergency landing in Nova Scotia.

We nearly reached the end of the runway when the pilot made a sharp, fast, left turn, and then throttled up as if we were taking off again. My face was pressed tight against the window to see what was going on, and then I saw another large plane coming down the same runway we had just left. I then understood what had happened and why.

"I'd trust this pilot to fly me anywhere," I said to Bonnie.

"He almost threw me out of my seat," Bonnie answered.

"Yeah, but another plane would have run into us if he hadn't," I explained to Bonnie.

After refueling, we were back in the air to New Jersey. I thanked the Lord and prayed for a safe flight home, and that I would find my car in one piece, in the long-stay parking lot.

This, along with Bonnie not being able to walk much in Spain because of her knee, were all we talked about during lunch at Hoss's after church on Sunday.

About a month after we had come back from Spain, I was in the church basement dusting for cobwebs, sweeping the basement floor, and cleaning the two classroom chairs and tables. As I mopped the lady's bathroom floor, I noticed on the paneled wall, at two separate locations, raised blister-like sections on the wall. One began six inches from the floor and continued up the wall nearly four feet high, and the other location, to the right of the vanity, began at floor level and continued about twelve inches up the wall.

Puzzled, I used my penknife and opened one blister to see if water was leaking into the wall. I peeled away an inch of paneling which revealed little white ant-like creatures crawling up and down in the wall. I then got a little baby food jar and forced three of the little white creatures into the jar, and then screwed the lid on the jar.

I took the jar to Henry's Pest Control to have the creatures identified. Mr. Henry told me they were subterranean termites, which lives about six feet underground. These were the workers who bring food to the queen, who will lay thousands of eggs in one day and never leaves the colony. I scheduled him to come for an inspection and treatment plan quote.

The quote came to $1200, of which, we had less than $30 in the church checking account. I showed the elders the evidence in the basement, and then started receiving special offerings to raise money for the treatment plan.

The first Sunday offering was less than $100. Week after week, a special fund offering was received, but at times I felt the church might get eaten by the termites before we would have funds enough to have them treated. Several weeks I went without paychecks to help add to the fund. Often, I thought, Why would a church ever enter into a building program, and get this far in debt without having funds set aside for emergencies?

When I took the pastorate of this church there were three mortgages on the church, and they had totally run out of money because most of the original people had left before I arrived. If it wasn't for outside jobs, my family and I felt like we would starve. But thanks to God, someone would always show up with food right after we had eaten our last meal on several occasions.

But even after paying off mortgages number two and three, offerings remained at bare minimums. On the other hand, since a lot of my outside jobs were done in members' homes, they always seemed to have enough money to finance their new renovations. Yet, if I preached a message similar to what Haggai preached, *"Is it time for you yourselves to be living in your paneled houses, while this house remains a ruin?"* Haggai 1:4 NIV, a few would stay out of church for weeks at a time, and their money would stay out of church with them.

After nearly six months, I finally was able to contract Henry's Pest Control, and have him treat for termites, after which, I had to redo the women's bathroom and two walls in the men's bathroom.

Two years later, I was working in the church basement chalking lines on the basement floor, to add a new Sunday school room. I removed a sheet of paneling to locate the two-by-four studding in order to secure a new wall, when I noticed more of those same termite mud tubes. I became furious. I was so angry that I threw my claw hammer down from the step ladder onto the floor so hard that it bounced half way up the wall and knocked a poster down. The poster slid down the wall over to my ladder, with these words facing me. I read from my elevated position: *"Trust in the Lord with all thine heart and lean not unto thine own understanding"* Proverbs 3:5 KJV.

I left the church and drove all the way to Conneaut, Ohio, before I cooled down, and then, only after pulling into

McDonald's and eating two cheeseburgers and a Diet Coke. Afterwards, I drove back and called Henry's Pest Control, explaining the new termite evidence.

He said, "There are probably several colonies since the church is so old." But he finally agreed to drill additional holes in the floor, and pump in more poison solution.

Those little white devils worked so much like Satan, in the dark avoiding the Light, that I preached several sermons titled: "Satan's activities." Especially since all their damage was done in darkness, just like the father of liars. They caused me to hate Satan more every day, giving him no doubt of my enmity toward him. God reminded me that "greater is He [Jesus] that is in me than he [Satan] that is in the world."

After the extra Sunday school room was finished, God sent in additional youth to fill it. Soon we needed access into the church for handicapped individuals.

Since Bob Friday was an elevator inspector, he suggested an elevator be installed, but it was so cost prohibitive that we gave up on that idea. One day as I stared at the back window in the sanctuary, I felt led to measure outside for a ramp. I talked this over with Don Darr and Bob Friday to get their opinions of replacing the window with a glass door and have a concrete ramp built to gain access from the outside into the sanctuary. They both agreed that I should proceed and get installation prices.

I sketched a drawing showing what the ramp might look like, and showed it to a concrete contractor. He said he was able to pour a "flat-bottomed, U-shaped" ramp, but he was unable to install the door nor the welded, metal railing, but told me he knew a man who could fabricate and weld the railing.

Since Bob's wife, Rosanne, had Multiple Sclerosis (MS), Bob offered to pay for the ramp, if the church would pay for the door. The men all agreed, and signed the contract to have the footer, block, and ramp poured.

The same day, I measured and calculated the height the ramp needed to be in order to be level with the sanctuary floor. I then drew a line on the outside brick with a blue Sharpie twelve inches wider than the door. The contractor scheduled to begin a week from Saturday.

After the ramp had dried for three weeks, we contracted Noyer's Welding Service to fabricate and install the railing, which after completion, was painted white to match the window frames. To save $1000 I sawed out the brick for the framing, built and installed the door frame, and contracted Parsons Penn Glass Company of Erie, to build and install the commercial, insulated, safety glass door.

Rosanne was able to drive her motorized wheel chair into the sanctuary and had the freedom to go anywhere she wished in the sanctuary or foyer.

One day I went into the sanctuary and sat on the front pew to pray. I stared at the outdated dark walnut paneling and said, "Lord, if I feel this depressed every time I look at all this brown, what does the congregation feel?"

That Sunday, I made my heartfelt feelings known to the congregation, how depressing our sanctuary looked from where they were sitting. Brown everywhere. I further reminded them that behind the second choir bench was still a large hole in the floor, covered with plywood, where the former pastor had begun to build a baptistery. "In its day," I said, "this paneling was probably the greatest in 1970, but I can't imagine me, being you, sitting where you sit and look at brown, brown, and more brown Sunday after Sunday."

Immediately after service my treasurer, informed me that we could not afford any more work in the church. He then quoted his version of Luke 14:28 to me, "The Bible says, 'we should sit down first, and count all the cost, to see if we have sufficient funds to finish it.'"

"Yes." I said. "The Bible also says, '*the just shall live by faith*'" Romans 1:17 KJV.

"I'm just saying," he quickly responded. "We can't afford to make any changes!"

"Could we afford the new ramp and new door?" I asked.

"That was Bob!" he answered. "And you know it."

"Was it?" I asked. "Or was it God, laying it on Bob's heart to do what he did for the church?"

He felt the church's money was his responsibility. I felt, and still feel, it is God's. So, I kept praying that God would open the church's eyes to what the Lord wanted.

Two weeks went by and Bob's son, Paul, was in town. He stopped down from New York to see the ramp his mom and dad had talked so much about, and to see his mom take her wheel chair to church by herself. We talked for a while, and then Paul said, "I want to do something special for the church. Is there anything you would like in the front?"

"Yes, a new chandelier in the foyer! This one is so dim, it barely makes any light," I said.

"I'm going to be home for a week. Go get one you like, and I'll pay whatever it costs," Paul said.

"Thank you so much, Paul."

"No. Thank you for thinking of Mom."

"Stop in before you go back to New York. As soon as I find something appropriate, I will install it. I want your approval before you go."

"Okay. That'll be great."

It didn't take me long to find the chandelier because I had already looked at one in Carpenter Electric's showroom several different times when purchasing other job supplies. I would sometimes visualize the appearance this light might make in our church foyer. I told the owner what had transpired between Paul and me, and he said, "Take it. Put it up. See if this is the one. I'll give you the bill to take with you."

"Thank you so much," I said. "Maybe you better add an extra bulb too."

"You got it. If it doesn't work out, bring it back."

"I think it will because I really like that chandelier."

That Sunday, as soon as Benny, my treasurer, walked in the front church door and saw the new light, he couldn't wait to question me. My only comment: "God gave it to us."

In addition to hearing the constant drum beat, "We can't afford this and we can't afford that," it had now been more than thirteen years, and I was still only receiving half the weekly pay that our Church Minutes authorized me to receive.

Benny had no problem paying church operating expenses out of the tithe fund rather than paying the pastor, who was essentially the church's first priority. This problem existed years before I accepted the pastorate because the church had paid utility bills, church insurance, etc. from the tithe fund because the offerings were always so low. But just because it had always been done this way, did not make it right, nor did it line up with what the church minutes ordained.

I felt impressed to begin preaching how *God loves a cheerful giver* two Sundays out of every month. In fact, on Wednesday nights, I taught two separate series on *Giving versus Receiving*. I went to the Bible book store and purchased every book I could find dealing with church giving to enhance my studies.

Benny complained weekly, now because "I only preached on money, money, money!"

The fact was, Benny was faithful in his tithes, but in addition to that, he rarely gave more than a dollar in the offering plate during any given service. I showed Benny, from Scripture, that tithes were already God's, not ours. God's 10 percent was never ours to keep, but He instructed us to give back to God what He said was His. And, if you only pay your tithes, you are not giving anything to God that is not already God's.

I went on to show Benny that God loves a cheerful giver. He was too frugal to accept this teaching, so after a few more weeks and much prayer, I asked Benny for his resignation, and for him to turn in all funds, check books, record books, reporting books and envelopes to the church Sunday morning.

He had everything pilled in one cardboard box which he handed to me Wednesday night before Bible study began. He then walked back out the church door, in a huff saying, "This is not over."

That night after church I went through the box to look at the last bank statement and compared the statement with the check book balance. The bank statement still showed a little more than $200 more than what the check book balance showed. I had asked Benny to find this error which had been carried over for more than three years, but he repeated, "I can't find a mistake anywhere." Everything else was in perfect order which confirmed Benny's honesty which I had never doubted. I just wanted our records to conform to the bank's records.

CHAPTER 10

THE RESOLUTION

A week later I received a call from Bishop Rodney Jeffords, my new State Overseer, whom I had just met at the state convention that year. He informed me that Mr. Benny Rumford had called, complaining that I had removed him from his long-held position.

"That is correct," I said. "I cannot use a person, in that position, who feels he has control of God's money."

"Brother Sines, I told him, quite frankly, that I back my pastors' decisions to run their churches the way they feel God's leading."

"Thank you, Brother Jeffords."

"He then threatened to call the General Overseer," Bishop Jeffords said. "I assured him, 'that was his right', and I even gave the Cleveland phone number to him."

"Wow! I guess I have a fight on my hands."

"I seriously doubt that, Brother Sines," Bishop Jeffords assured me. "You keep doing what you feel God desires. Your track record looks good to me."

Only three weeks after Benny's departure, God impressed upon me that it was time to move forward with the sanctuary renovation. There were only ten dollars in the general fund checking account, but God still urged me to move forward. I grabbed a pad of small-block graph paper from the office, my 25' tape measure, a sharp pencil, and went into the sanctuary to lay out what God was showing me.

I visualized a ceiling beam, 12-inches high by 8-inches thick and 30-feet long, all the way across the front stage area, which would finish flush to the ceiling, and flush on each end with the existing walls. This beam would enable a new ceiling to be installed above the stage because the last five rows of the existing ceiling tiles were sagging due to the weight of blown-in insulation above. As soon as I re-measured where the beam was to fit, I left to talk with my friend, Dan, at Kraft Lumber on Peninsula Drive.

Dan assured me they could fabricate the 30-foot beam using four two by twelve's, with one half-inch plywood sandwiched in between each two by twelve, to keep it from sagging. When he told me he could have it delivered in a week, I called Don Darr and Bob Friday, who both said, "Go for it." I hung up Dan's phone and gave him the go-ahead to proceed.

I drove back to the church to finish calculating the amount of drywall and the framing materials needed for the choir risers. I was excited to be moving on this project, knowing I was being obedient to God, and being assured He would provide everything we needed as we needed it.

I ordered a large dumpster from Waste Management, to be placed between Brown Avenue and the sidewalk. Every available man in the church pitched in to help tear out the old paneling and debris, which took nearly a week in itself.

Kraft Lumber delivered the beam Saturday morning at eight o'clock. It took four of us guys to unload and carry the beam into the sanctuary. We had already put the scaffolding in place, so as soon as Brian got home from work that afternoon, he, Richard, Roger, and I lifted the beam onto the scaffolding, one end at a time. God only, knows how much this beam weighed, but nevertheless among the four of us, we managed to set it into the concrete openings which I hewed out of the cement pillars on each side of the sanctuary. There were several high-fives given in the sanctuary that day. Once in place, we all felt an elephant could hang from this beam. I tightened the beam in place with a sledge hammer, driving steel rods underneath, and mixed up mortar, and filled every gap. No one could miss the excitement on these young faces as to what God was doing.

Money starting coming in from people whom we never imagined it would come from. I don't mean dollar offerings either, although we never turned a single dollar down, but it was not abnormal to receive $500 to $1000 dollar checks, earmarked, "sanctuary renovation," on any given Sunday. One man, who did not want his name known or any publicity, by himself chose to buy a new sign and have it installed in the front yard, if I would agree to make permanent on the sign, *"Everyone has been called."* The sign wasn't even part of the projected renovation, but we were all following what God wanted.

"The Great Commission," I assured him, "means every single person, so I certainly have no problem with the wording."

The sign, which cost more than $7000, wasn't even part of the renovation project, but it was paid in full on the day of installation. This same man agreed to pay one-half the cost to have the entire church and the new choir area carpeted. It never ceases to amaze me how God always finds people willing to give to causes, He ordains.

Before we laid out the choir walls and ceiling, I had the owner of Grise audio-visual Center come to the church and give his professional opinion how to properly angle both the walls and ceiling to best project the sound. We followed his design suggestions to the inch, but later, God added the lighted cross in the center. I say, "God added," because the gentleman insisted we install a custom-made $5000 leaded-glass cross, created by Erie's local mosaic glass artist, John Vahanian. The unnamed gentleman paid the entire bill himself.

The entire renovation exceeded $23,000, but when the last coat of paint was applied, and carpet installed, everything was paid in full. The church had accrued no debt for any part of the sanctuary renovation or the disability ramp installation.

Church attendance bounced up and down from 45 and 85, depending on the calendar month, but wouldn't remain at the high end due to limited street parking, and the fact that we were an inner-city church. The trend in Erie is like many other cities in the United States. Churches around our city which was built at least a mile outside the city limits grew somewhere between four hundred and twelve hundred in Sunday's attendance.

I thought about relocating many times, but never received the slightest confirmation from God to make a move. Yes, I looked at several different locations, all outside of Erie, but never felt God in any of them. So, to enhance our parking we elected to remove a tree and pour a three-car disabled parking area between the sidewalk and Brown Avenue.

The off-street parking was certainly appreciated by a few elderly members, although it required us to hire snow removal service twice per week, each winter.

A couple snow-birds, would spend their winters in Florida.

Rossane Friday, known to everyone as "Rosey," purchased a dozen different colored roses from Jackson and Perkins, in Michigan, and had them shipped, to be planted all along the 22nd Street side of the church.

Our sound system has gone through several metamorphisms over the years. We advanced, from one original microphone and public address (PA) system, to an eight-channel mixer, amp, and used prerecorded cassette tapes for the choir to sing with. Then, after cassette tapes gave way to CDs, we had a complete sound room built with a 32-channel Yamaha mixer, two Samson amps, a frequency synchronizer, two new Yamaha floor monitors and two wall-mounted Yamaha speakers, and several new microphones. The entire sound-system was installed for $7500.

A few years later we added a state-of-the-art media system, consisting of two computers, two 70-inch LED high definition TVs, (one on the back wall for the choir and the other centered on the beam above the podium for the congregation). To this we added power point and video software, the fastest video card available, 450 feet of Cat-5 cable, and mounting hardware all installed for an additional cost of $13,000.

God is not poor nor is He cheap. In addition to the media and sound system, God also blessed us over the years, with a Yamaha Clavinova piano, a Korg Triton Le workstation key board, a Pearl 9-piece drum set, an acrylic podium with the Church of God emblem engraved on the front, with a matching water stand, and all items were newly purchased. In addition, all the pews were padded and covered. And still, the church remains debt free.

God allowed all this to happen so His servants might continue to minister to His children, their families, and friends in the city of Erie.

While all this was being accomplished in the church, God also blessed Pastor and Bonnie with a home of their own, adjacent to the church front steps.

I had been taking care of Connie and George Smithers from the year 2000 to 2004. She was eighty-eight and he was ninety. Many times I would answer the phone, and it would be Connie begging me to come over and help George up off the floor or to test his sugar or to get him to stop swearing at Connie. He would often take his insulin shot, and then fall asleep in his chair without eating. I would hustle over from time to time, and do whatever I needed to do to assist.

On several occasions, I had to spoon feed George orange juice in order to elevate his sugar. Another time I picked him up from between the bed and the wall, and stayed with him until I was sure he was okay. The worst was finding him in his underwear, standing in his own feces, in the middle of the kitchen. I led him to the bathroom and had him sit on the toilet while I filled a pan with warm water to wash his feet.

"I know Jesus washed his disciples' feet," I said to George. "But I don't think he washed any of this from between their toes."

Connie would always ask, "Pastor how can we ever repay you for all you do?"

One day I answered, "Put me in your will to have the first option to buy your home."

"How much," Connie asked.

"How much did you pay for it?"

"$30,000."

"Would you take $40,000?" I asked. "You and George talk it over, if you're serious."

About a month later Connie called and said, "Pastor, do you have a couple minutes? I have someone I want you to meet."

"Sure. I'll be right over."

Their attorney, Ronald Soutter was sitting at the kitchen table with her and George. "Please meet our lawyer," she said motioning for me to have a seat.

"Ronald Soutter. You're the Pastor across the street?"

"Yes. Pastor Sines."

"Mr. and Mrs. Smithers wish to include you in their will, giving you the first option to buy their home for $40,000. Is this right?"

"Yes," I answered.

"Then, I need you to sign all eight copies on the blank spaces I have marked."

"This of course depends if I can get financing," I said nervously.

"This only gives you the option to buy. It's not a contract to buy," said Mr. Soutter.

"Thank you both very much," I said, shaking George and Connie's hand. "And thank you, Mr. Soutter."

I left their home feeling God working in my favor. As I crossed the street to the parsonage, I immediately I remembered telling God, "I didn't need a hundred houses, but He owed me one."

Later that winter, I received a call from a nurse at the Millcreek Community Hospital informing me that Connie had congestive heart failure. I quickly changed clothes and drove to the hospital. I went straight to the ICU room where she lay.

"Connie! Pastor Sines. Can you hear me?"

Her eyes were wide open, but focused somewhere beyond me. I called for the nurse to come over, but the nurse said,

"That's the way she's been for the past hour. I called you because she had you listed as her Pastor."

I prayed with Connie, but received no response. She looked so scared. I then prayed for her salvation, hoping she could possibly hear me, and ask Jesus' forgiveness. I couldn't help but think of the many times I had invited her to church, but her response was always, "No, I'm Catholic." Even though I explained to her, that more than 50 percent of the people in our church were former Catholics.

The hospital later told me she passed a few hours after I left that January night. I pray she was able to spend the time in her mind, talking with Jesus.

I called Connie's house keeper, Diane, to see if she could spend the night with George. She told me, "a night or two, but you'll have to make arrangements for him to be in a home."

Since I was made their Power of Attorney and Executor, I knew the responsibility fell on my shoulders, so I assured Diane that I would try to find somewhere suitable for George tomorrow if possible. Diane had the phone numbers of the daughters and son, so she told me that she would tell them about their mom. She dreaded even talking with them, almost as much as I dreaded doing the funeral. How could anybody forsake their parents, no matter how bad they got along?

I knew George was a former Navy man, so I decided to check out Sunrise Assisted Living at Presque Isle Bay because of the excellent view overlooking the Bay. They had only one opening, so I signed all the papers for George to be brought their tomorrow afternoon. He was used to riding in the Ambulance, so I made arrangements for them to pick him up, right after I brought in his night stand, lamp, dresser and his clothes.

I showed George the view of the Bay from the dining room, and he seemed to like it quite well. I then gave his caretaker his meds, his doctor's name, and instructed them that he always preferred going to the Millcreek Community Hospital, even though Hamot Hospital was just down the street. They also assured me that they would bring him to the funeral parlor during visiting hours, and bring him back.

I left the two daughters pick the casket because the son wanted no part of anything. The daughter's attitudes reeked of hatred, which was made visible when they both insisted on the lowest grade casket. The funeral director just looked at me and rolled her eyes. Thank God I had prepared the director for what might transpire with this family when I first made the arrangements. I was also grateful the grave plots were picked out and purchased many years ago.

I no sooner said my closing remarks at the funeral service and gave the final prayer, when the grandson blurted out, "How soon can we get into my granddad's house?"

"I'll let everyone know as soon as I talk to Attorney Soutter," I said. "But I know he doesn't have office hours on weekends."

I called Attorney Soutter Monday morning and informed him that family members wanted to take things out of the house that was willed to them, and that I had already taken hundreds of digital photos.

He said, "Pastor, if they are all there at the same time, read the will aloud and make sure the Will, is followed to the letter, for the items marked.

"What about after all the items in the Will are dispersed?" I asked.

"Again, as long as they are all there, it will save you from taking an inventory if you let them clean house, except for the appliances that are all mentioned in the will which stay with the house."

I called everyone in the family and informed them that the house would be open at nine o'clock Saturday morning, and reminded them, that every family member had to be present.

Once the specific items were signed off according to the will, and taken to their vehicles, I said, "Now, as long as you all agree on who gets what, I don't care if you remove everything except the washer, dryer, gas stove, refrigerator, and humidifier. These appliances remain with the house."

Almost immediately, the house looked like it had been attacked by vultures. Before I would allow anyone to leave with their booty, I had each person stack the items they had confiscated into a pile, and then I took pictures of them standing behind their loot. By evening, the only thing left was a metal porch swing on the front porch, which was gone sometime before I got out of bed the next morning.

George told me he had seen his family more in the last week than he had in ten years. I visited him nearly every day. I loaded up 15 large boxes of Depends, which were left in George's basement, and donated them to Sunrise. The director was really grateful because she told me that these were smaller than what they had in stock.

After only four weeks the director called and told me that George had to be rushed to the Millcreek Community Hospital. His blood pressure had gotten dangerously low. I called his son and daughters, then I went to the hospital to check on George and to pray with him. He was very alert and responsive, and thanked me for praying for him.

The next morning, I was shocked when the hospital called and said he had passed through the night. I called his family, who each repeated, "He was doing good last night. We all sang, *'Take us out to the Ball Game,'* and he sang right along with us."

That was the most love they showed their father since this all began. The hospital chief of staff asked me if I wanted an autopsy performed. I said, "Why? He was 92 years old."

He died exactly 30 days after his wife had passed. I was so grateful that George had experienced one final time of joy with his family before he went to meet the Lord.

What a change from mother to father, the son and both daughters picked George's casket. The casket alone had a $10,000 price tag. And, at the end of the funeral service they all sang, *"Take us out to the Ball Game."* I felt God finally broke through to this family.

Bonnie and I applied for a VA loan, as soon as Veterans Affairs informed me that I was eligible to receive a second VA loan, with zero money down at a 5.5% interest rate. We closed on our new home, Monday, April 18, 2005, the day after my sixtieth birthday. After signing all the papers, Bonnie and I spent a few moments in the car, just thanking and praising the Lord, before leaving for lunch on the way "home."

The very next day I rented a large dumpster from Waste Management, and had it placed along the curb in front of the house. Richard, his friend Albert, and I carried out all the leftover trash from the house, and removed the temporary basement walls, shelving, quilting rags, box after box of craft materials, and every unusable thing left by the Smithers family. One dumpster wasn't enough so I ordered a second, and filled it as well. I ended up ordering a third because the seller was responsible for all removal costs, everything the buyer did not want left in the house or garage.

Over the next year and a half, I maxed out my Lowes and Home Depot cards, by totally renovating the house with new windows, doors, plumbing, electrical wiring, and had a Lennox high efficient furnace/heat pump with central air installed, which I financed with a $7000 signature loan through the G. E. Federal Credit Union. Every time Bonnie brought me over a cup of hot coffee, I apologized for the mess usually on the floor or in the area I was working. She kept saying, "I don't care how much mess you create now, but after we move in—no more messes."

It was mid-September 2006, when we finally made the move, immediately after Cohen's Carpeting finished installing our Berber carpet. Carrying furniture across the street proved to be very tiring, so we took the larger items first. We would make a few trips, rest, and then place furniture in their proper areas. We continued this cycle until all heavy items were moved and arranged. Smaller items were moved over as needed.

The first night, in our new home, Bonnie and I felt like we were on our second honeymoon, although it had taken two weeks before it sank in that we were not in a motel. It felt good again, having a home of our own. Bonnie shared that night, the years of anxiety living in the parsonage, knowing if something happened to me, she would have to find a place to live within weeks.

Together, we scheduled a housewarming, backyard cookout for the second Saturday in October. We invited everyone in church, the neighbors on our street, our District Overseer and his wife, and two other Erie minister friends of mine and their wives. We owe everything to God for what we now had, and we wanted to give an expression of appreciation to the church, and our neighbors, to show how God remains faithful to His servants.

We set up the church's large tent in our backyard, carried over all the folding chairs from the church, and six tables. Bonnie and I furnished Smith hotdogs, buns, paper plates, plastic silverware, sodas, and ice. She asked all the ladies to bring covered dishes.

Before the day was over, I had counted 114 people who had expressed their love to us, and each of them wished blessings upon us as well. As I look back over the 30 plus years, I see how God has remained faithful to us both. And, I know God will do the same for all His disciples because I now realize how true it is, *"that God does not show favoritism, but accepts men from every nation who fear him and do what is right"* Acts 10:34-35 NIV.

CHAPTER 11

THE REWARD

There are no rewards that are truly meaningful in this lifetime. I understand that many people seek some type of reward for their hard work and labors, but please, be aware, there is no reward man can ever attain in this lifetime that can even come close to what God has already promised.

All the way back in the beginning of the Bible, God promises, *"I am your shield, your very great reward"* Genesis 15:1 NIV.

He ends with the same promise in the very last chapter, *"Behold, I am coming soon! My reward is with me, and I will give to everyone according to what he has done"* Revelation 22:12 NIV.

If you think about it, what could possibly be more rewarding for any man or woman, at the end of life, then to hear Jesus say, *"Well done, good and faithful servant! You have been faithful with a few things; I will put you in charge of many things? Come and share your master's happiness!"* Matthew 25:23 NIV

If we seek earthly rewards, our seeking is in vain, but if we seek heavenly rewards, we will enjoy them throughout eternity. I have never been richer in all my life than I am right now. My prayer is that you too, will choose the better. Amen.